Encourage The Young Women

Berceuse (Lullaby, 1875)
William-Adolphe Bouguereau (1825-1905)

Encourage The Young Women
Come, let us reason the Scripture together

Ety Wilson

Kikobian Books
www.kikobian.com

Encourage The Young Women by Ety Wilson
© 2014 by Leigh Tate
Cover photo © 2008 by Leigh Tate

All rights reserved. No part of this publication may be reproduced, distributed, or transmitted in any form or by any means, including photocopying, recording, copying and pasting, or any other electronic or mechanical methods, without the prior written permission of the publisher, except in the case of brief quotations embodied in critical reviews and certain other noncommercial uses permitted by copyright law. For information, contact Kikobian Books, info@kikobian.com.

Scripture quotations taken from the New American Standard Bible®, Copyright © 1960, 1962, 1963, 1968, 1971, 1972, 1973, 1975, 1977, 1995 by The Lockman Foundation. Used by permission (www.Lockman.org).

Edited by Heather East

This book was built from the ground up with open source software on an open source operating system: Ubuntu Linux 12.04 (Precise Pangolin), Xfce 4.10 Desktop Environment, LibreOffice 3.5.7.2 Writer word processor, Gnumeric Spreadsheet 1.10.17, Zim 0.54 desktop wiki, Leafpad 0.8.18.1 text editor, Gimp 2.8 photo editor, Inkscape 0.48 vector drawing program, Evince Document Viewer 3.4.0, PDF-Shuffler 0.6.0, and Scribus 1.4 and 1.5 desktop publisher. Also used were open source fonts Alex Brush Regular, Ezra SIL Regular, GFS Didot Classic Regular, Linden Hill Regular, Linden Hill Italic (all licensed under the SIL Open Font License, Version 1.1), and Liberation Sans Italic (licensed under GNU Public License v.2).

ISBN 978-0-9897111-1-1

Kikobian Books
www.kikobian.com

Now these were more noble-minded than those in Thessalonica, for they received the word with great eagerness, examining the Scriptures daily to see whether these things were so.

Acts 17:11

Contents

Frontispiece ii
Preface xi

Introduction

The Holy Bible: Word of God? Or Word of Man? 3
How Do You Read The Bible? 7
The Word of God: A Reasonable Approach 9
Definition of a Christian 15

Titus 2:3-5

The Women of Titus Chapter 2 19
Whom Do You Admire? 23
How To Do A Word Study 25
Who Are The Older Women? 29
Older Women Likewise: Women in Christian Leadership . . 31
Temperance: For Drunks Only? 33
Dignity: A Basic Human Right? 37
Being Sensible 41
Spiritual Soundness 45
Is Faith Blind? 47
Faith is an Action Word 51
Love: More Than a Feeling? 53
Circumstances Getting You Down? 57
Why Me? Persevering Through Difficulties 59
Behavior Check for Women in Christian Leadership 63
How Many Kinds of Gossip Are There, Anyway? 67
Nor Enslaved To Much Wine 71
The Problem With Being Good 75
Teaching What Is Good 77
How Not to Encourage Your Friends and Family 79

To Love Their Husbands 83
To Love Their Children 87
What Do You Want for Your Children? 91
Children, Sin, and the D Word 93
Why I Homeschooled My Children 97
Public Education: Children as Missionaries 101
Are Some Sins Worse Than Others? 103
Guardians of the Household 107
Influencing Others 111
Feminism's 4-Letter Word 115
Submission For Husbands? You've Got to be Kidding 119
Submission: Biblical Inequality? 123
Changing Our Husbands 125
Submission: Where Do We Draw the Line? 129
Submission To Whom? 131
Dishonoring the Word of God 133
"That She Respect Her Husband" 139
The Spiritually Mature Woman:
   A Summary of Titus 2:3-5 143

Genesis Chapters 1 - 3

Genesis 1: An Overview of Creation 149
Genesis 2: Filling in The Details 151
Leaving and Cleaving 155
Companionship in Marriage 159
Help Meet 163
Genesis 3 : So What Happened? 167
Deceived 171
The Consequences 175
The Problem With Sin 181
Being a Godly Woman 183

Proverbs 31:10-31

The Excellent Woman: By Whose Definition?	187
A Woman's Power	189
A Husband's Trust	191
Willingly Industrious	195
Diligent Provider	197
Organized Manager	199
Shrewd Investor	203
Woman of Strength	207
Financially Sensible	211
Skilled With Her Hands	217
Philanthropist	221
Faithfully Prepared	225
Takes Care Of Her Appearance	229
Unity in Marriage	233
Successful Businesswoman	237
No Fear	239
Wise Teacher	243
Cause and Effect	247
Kingdom Minded	251
The Excellent Woman: A Summary of Proverbs 31:10-31	255
Conclusion	259
Bibliography and Resources	261

Indices

General Index	265
Word Study Index	277
Scripture Index	279

Preface

I suppose it could be said that, technically, this book began as a weblog entitled "Encourage The Young Women."[1] Its groundwork, however, was laid many years before.

After my daughter was born 30 years ago, I became what is now called a stay-at-home mom, or SAHM. Of course, back then, the acronym hadn't been thought of yet. "Stay-at-home mom," yes, although I thought of it more broadly as "homemaker." I was strongly influenced by my godly grandmother's example and had a bend toward the domestic arts. Plus, being socially awkward, I have always been more comfortable at home. I'm a homebody.

But deeper than that, I have always had a conviction that children should be raised at home, by their mothers primarily, but by their fathers too. Through their different roles, both parents provide a framework and nurturing environment in which children can thrive and mature.

Three years later my son was born. Somehow we survived the preschool years. I worked two days a week at our church's Mothers-Day-Out program. When it was time for my daughter to start school, I wish I could say that I started homeschooling right from the beginning. But I didn't. We did start with a Christian school, because I had a firm conviction about Christian education. In fact, it wasn't until several years later that I met my first homeschool mom. I was curious, but not convinced. She was enthusiastic, but not pushy. Even so, she planted a seed.

The fruit of that seed was eleven years of homeschooling. We homeschooled all the way through high school graduation, and both my children went on to college.

It was during those college years when they were first away from home that I discovered something. I realized that my time without them was more difficult than all my years of childrearing. Not that those years were easy! But they gave me purpose. And as much as I looked forward to pursuing my other interests after my children were grown up and on their own, it just wasn't the same. I felt fortunate that they were still close enough for us to spend vacations and holidays as a family. Yet, I realized that our relationship needed to change. The parent/child relationship needed to grow and mature as they did.

In spite of that, it took a while to see myself as having an empty nest. Not that I didn't fill it with busyness. I am still a homemaker - a keeper at home. But I had more time on my hands and longed for a sense of purpose again.

I prayed about this for several years: prayed about getting a job, finishing my master's degree, volunteering somewhere, or starting a home business. None of these settled well in my spirit. One day, Titus 2:3-5 came to mind.

> Older women likewise are to be reverent in their behavior, not malicious gossips, nor enslaved to much wine, teaching what is good, that they may encourage the young women to love their husbands, to love their children, to be sensible, pure, workers at home, kind, being subject to their own husbands, that the word of God may not be dishonored.

I wasn't sure if I knew how to do all that. In fact, I knew I didn't. But I could take the Scripture, apply the Bible study techniques I had been taught, and share what I learned. I could share what I've experienced and how the Lord dealt with me through it. How He guided and taught me. Perhaps in some small way, I could encourage others.

I started blogging in February 2008. When the Lord stopped giving me the lessons, I stopped writing. Several years later I felt His prompting to turn the blog into a book, and here it is.

[1]https://encouragetheyoungwomen.wordpress.com/

Introduction

The Holy Bible: Word of God? Or Word of Man?

I'm guessing that no book has generated more controversy or more argument over the ages than the book entitled The Holy Bible. Did God write it? Did men write it? Is it a book of suggestions? Opinions? Dos and don'ts? Is it historically accurate? Is it culturally relevant? Is it open to interpretation?

Everybody believes something. And everyone has a basis for their beliefs, whether about God, life and death, our purpose in life, or the world in general. Most of us have an idea of what we believe, but how many of us know the basis for our beliefs?

Much of the argument over the Bible revolves around who wrote it. As an authoritative source, it is often dismissed on the basis of authorship: "I don't believe in the Bible because it was written by men." My husband, who is an evangelist, encounters this frequently. He often responds by asking, "Well, what do you believe?" Every single person with whom he has had this conversation must inevitably resource their beliefs with something of human authorship. This seems more than a little ironic if that person rejects the Bible for the same reason. So what's the problem?

I think it all boils down to this: If the Bible is written by God, then when I read it I am faced with a choice. I either have to accept that it is true or not. If I accept it as true, then I have to admit that I am wrong about things, and some of these things are very personal.

Human nature doesn't like to be wrong. Nor does it like to feel twinges of guilt. Nor does it want to change. The easiest solution therefore, is to find a basis for rejecting the Bible as truth. Declaring it to be the writings and opinions of men is one common basis for that rejection. If I can convince myself of human authorship for the Bible, then I don't have to face any other "truth" than the one I have chosen for myself.

For the Christian, on the other hand, having a book written by God Himself (through the agency of men inspired by the Holy Spirit), is both an encouragement and a comfort. By giving me specific information about my world and specific instructions for living in it, I gain a considerable amount of freedom. I am no longer burdened with having to make behavioral decisions about situations, nor am I faced with the consequences of acting on my own reasoning or impulses. Granted, following God's way isn't always easy, but it does give me a consistent standard for living.

But how do I know that I'm right about what the Bible says? Isn't its truth different for every person? Doesn't it depend upon my own personal situation? Doesn't it depend on how I'm feeling about things? Consider this illustration: Suppose you were to write a letter to me about a dog named Jessica. Then suppose that my sister picked it up, glanced through it, and started telling folks that you were calling our friend Jessica a dog. Would you just shrug it off by saying, "Oh well, that's just her interpretation"? I doubt it. I should think that you would want to set the record straight to avoid a misunderstanding; especially if our friend Jessica became angry about it. Rather, you had written to a specific person with something specific in mind.

So consider this. The Bible has a specific author, who dictated a specific message to specific people. The Almighty knew exactly what He meant when He inspired men to write, and He meant what He said to be accurately understood. That being the case, wouldn't it be prudent for a reader to not be too careless in his or her interpretations? Wouldn't it be wise to not make assumptions about what is meant? God had specific things in mind when the Bible was written. The job of reader then, is to accurately interpret what God is saying. The problem is that there is more than one way to approach this.

Interestingly, all the supposed contradictions in the Bible can be resolved with the correct method of interpretation, which we'll take a look at next.

How Do You Read The Bible?

When I first became a Christian I fell in love with reading my Bible. I set aside time every day with my cup of morning coffee to read it. It was alive to me, and personal. My time with the Lord was such a highlight in my day so that eventually I couldn't have a cup of coffee without feeling that I should be reading my Bible.

I have to admit that immediately after my conversion I really wasn't sure if the entire Bible was true and reliable. I certainly accepted the Gospels, because these were the life and words of Jesus, the God for whom I had searched so long. The rest of it I wasn't sure about. I can't put my finger on how or when I came to understand the whole book to be the Word of God. What I can tell you is that everything changed for me when I learned how to study it.

One of the things I realized was that previously, I hadn't actually been studying the Bible; I'd been scanning it. My Bible was full of underlined passages that spoke to me, but when I learned how to study God's Word, it became alive in a way I'd never known possible. At that point I lost all interest in television, books, and movies; studying the Bible became the most fascinating thing in my life. I felt as though I had gone from simply walking through the Word and picking up nuggets of gold, to digging deep and mining gold for myself.

Basically, there are two ways to approach the Bible. The most common is to see what others say about the Bible through commentaries, handbooks, preachers, teachers, scientists, the latest book from the Christian bookstore, etc. There can be value in this, yet look at what Luke writes:

> *And the brethren immediately sent Paul and Silas away by night to Berea; and when they arrived, they went to the*

> *synagogue of the Jews. Now these were more noble-minded than those in Thessalonica, for they received the word with great eagerness, examining the Scriptures daily, to see whether it was so.* Acts 17:10-11

Notice, it doesn't say that they received the word with great eagerness and then discussed it amongst themselves to see how they felt about it. Nor does it say they sought others' opinions about it, looked to their commentaries, or researched whether or not there was scientific evidence to back it up. Rather, the Bereans were called noble-minded because they used the Scriptures as the standard for judging what Paul and Silas said. I don't know about you, but I would certainly rather be classified as "noble-minded" than what the opposite implies.

The second approach is to let the Bible speak for itself. It begins with the Bible and uses the Bible as its own commentary. Rather than asking, "What do others say about the Bible?" it asks, "What does the Bible say about the Bible?" This method is a bit more scientific in its approach. By that, I mean that it uses specific principles to read, interpret, and apply Scripture. This method can be applied to any book of the Bible without a formal study guide. I'll give you a rundown next.

The Word of God: A Reasonable Approach

How do we let the Bible speak for itself?

> "It shall greatly helpe ye
> to understand Scripture
> if thou mark
> not only what is spoken
> or wrytten
> but of whom
> and to whom
> with what words
> at what time
> where,
> to what intent
> with what circumstances
> consider what goeth before
> and what followeth."
> Miles Coverdale, 1535

Hermeneutics is the principles, method, and practice of interpretation. There are books upon books written on this subject, analyzing and arguing the correct method. The method I use I learned by taking Precept Upon Precept[1] classes, although I also studied it through a seminary course I once took. Miles Coverdale summarized it quite nicely.

The process is one of asking the Scripture questions. Consider that if God wants us to grow in grace and knowledge (2 Peter 3:18), then He is not afraid of our questions and is more than willing to answer them.

It begins with prayer. It begins by asking the Lord to help you lay aside what you think the Scripture means, and to see it through fresh eyes, without any preconceptions. Some of my favorite Scriptures to pray are:

> 2 Cor. 10:5 – That the Lord will destroy speculations and wrong ideas about His Word
>
> John 16:13 – That the Holy Spirit will guide me in all truth
>
> Psalm 119:18 – To open my eyes to behold wonderful things from His word

The questions we ask Scripture follow a process:
1. Observation – asks , "What does it say?"
2. Interpretation – asks, "What does it mean?"
3. Application – asks, "What difference does it make?"

OBSERVATION – What does it say?

This is not as easy to do as you'd think. Most of us make assumptions about the meaning of what we read and hear. The human tendency seems to be to interpret before actually understanding what is being said. The role of observation is to give the writer/speaker a fair hearing.

One of the goals of observation is to discover the big picture. This in turn, gives us the context for everything that was written. For example, suppose you were to walk into a room and overhear bits of a conversation between friends. You catch, "Sam" and "What a turkey." What are they talking about?

a. Sam's prize winning Narragansett at the state fair?
b. Thanksgiving dinner at Sam's?
c. Sam's three strikes in a row at Friday night bowling?
d. That Sam is a dope?

Whether or not you chose the correct answer would depend upon how well you knew Sam and this group's

The Word of God: A Reasonable Approach

recent activities. In other words, you would need to know the *context* in which the statement was being made.

To discover the big picture and determine context, we read with a purpose. Like any good investigative reporter, we look for the who, what, when, where, why, and how of the text. For example:

Who? – Who wrote it? To whom is it written? Who are the major characters? Who is being discussed?

What? – What type of literature is it? (Historical? Biographical? Poetry? Prophecy? A teaching? A letter?) Is it literal? Figurative? What is the author's purpose in writing? What are the main ideas? What are the author's circumstances? What are the recipients' circumstances? What questions are they asking? What problems do they have? What outcome is expected?

Where? – Where is the author? Where are the recipients? From where are they coming? To where are they going?

When? – When is it being written? When did the events take place, or have they yet? When do characters speak? When is something supposed to happen?

Why? – Why is the author writing? Why are these topics being addressed? Why is a particular idea being mentioned? Why are specific characters choosing their particular courses of action?

How? – How did the situation occur? How do the characters deal with it? How does the author know what he does? How can his solution be accomplished?

The questions will vary depending upon the actual passage, and some questions don't have answers.

INTERPRETATION - What does it mean?

Once the context and major topics have been determined, it becomes easier to interpret them accurately. Based on the principle that the Bible is the best authority on the Bible, objective interpretation assumes that the Bible never contradicts itself. If it appears to, then the interpreter digs deeper. The tools of interpretation include word studies and cross references.

Word studies help us to not assume a word's meaning - for example, the word "love." Think about how we use it in the English language. I can love God, my country, my husband, my children, baseball, and chocolate cake. One word covers all. From the context, you decide which type of love I'm talking about. The Bible also uses the word "love" (charity) in different contexts. But Greek, in which the New Testament was written, has four distinct words for "love": *agape* – unconditional love; *philos* (also *philia* or *phileo*) – love amongst friends; *storge* – love of family; and *eros* – physical attraction. How do we know which one is meant in a particular passage of Scripture? By doing a word study.

Cross referencing uses the Bible as its own commentary. These tell us what else the Bible has to say on a particular word or topic, and how those words might be used. A good concordance is a useful tool for this.

After doing word studies and cross referencing, we can take a look at other translations and commentaries. You may even find that, based on your own study, you don't necessarily agree with them. The important thing is to be able to back up your own interpretation with Scripture, and not what someone else says about Scripture.

The Word of God: A Reasonable Approach

APPLICATION – What difference does it make?

Application takes the truths seen through observation and interpretation, and does something about them. It seeks to discover how the verse or passage being studied is personally relevant. As Paul puts it:

> *All Scripture is inspired by God and profitable for <u>doctrine</u>, for <u>reproof</u>, for <u>correction</u>, for <u>training in righteousness</u>; that the man of God may be adequate, equipped for every good work.* 2 Timothy 3:16 – 17

Application then, looks at the Scripture for:

Doctrine – What truth is the Lord trying to teach me here? Is there a principle to be applied to my life?

Reproof – Are there errors in my thoughts, attitudes, motives, or actions that need to be corrected?

Correction – Is there something in my life of which I need to repent or ask forgiveness?

Training in righteousness – Are there any commands, promises, warnings, exhortations, or examples for me to heed and follow?

For a more in-depth description of how to study your Bible, I would recommend the following:

Basic Bible Interpretation, Roy B. Zuck, Victor Books, Wheaton, IL, 1991
How To Study Your Bible, Kay Arthur, Harvest House Publishers, Eugene, OR, 1994
Understanding and Applying the Bible, J. Robertson McQuilkin, Moody Press, Chicago, 1983

Definition of a Christian

There is one more thing I would like to address before we begin this study. It is a term I use frequently throughout the book and it is important enough that I think it deserves clarification. It is a definition of the word, "Christian".

Over the years I have learned that when different people say, "I'm a Christian," they all don't necessarily mean the same thing. The term "Christian" is commonly used, but unfortunately, the label doesn't mean a whole lot these days in terms of defining actual beliefs. It has other, assumed meanings. For some it means church membership or having responded to an alter call; for others it's their family heritage, and for others it means a changed life in Jesus Christ. In addition, various churches, denominations, and groups don't define the term the same way. Does it mean having been baptized into a particular church or denomination, or being a member of a larger Christian community regardless of doctrine? Does it mean being a follower of Christ the Enlightened Master, or Christ the Son of God?

In our homeschool group, we had one mom who accepted anything under the label of Christian: books, curricula, music, magazines, etc. As I watched her and her children over the years, I realized that a lot of things labeled Christian didn't look any different than what the rest of the world was offering. It seemed as though the label was simply a marketing ploy to sell more product to a particular group of people. That was a good experience though, as it caused me to look more closely at everything using that label.

It is not my goal to turn this book into a philosophical thesis or doctrinal debate. I do think it's important that since I use the term, you, the Reader, should know what I mean when I use it. To me, the bottom line as to whether or not one is a "true Christian" all boils down to how one answers two simple questions:

Who is Jesus?
What are you going to do about it?

When I use the term "Christian," I am referring to one who believes that Jesus Christ is the only Son of God, and has made the choice to repent of their sin and follow Jesus. I realize some may want to add other qualifiers, but the bottom line is how one answers these two questions. These are the women to whom I am writing.

Titus 2:3-5

The Women of Titus Chapter 2

I want to begin by taking look at the book of Titus. As we read through Titus and begin the process of observation, we ask the text, "Who?" As we read, we look for *who* is mentioned in the text. We see that it was written by the Apostle Paul to Titus, a fellow worker for the gospel. We also see that Paul mentions seven groups of people: elders (overseers), deceivers, older men, older women, young women, young men, and bondslaves.

Another important question we need to ask is, "Why?" Why did Paul write this letter? In Titus 1:5 we get an idea of Paul's purpose.

> *For this reason I left you in Crete, that you might set in order what remains, and appoint elders in every city as I directed you.* Titus 1:5

The first two groups of people mentioned, elders and deceivers, point back to Paul's instruction to appoint elders in every city. The other five groups are the reason for his instruction to set the new body of believers in order. An important theme of Titus deals with how individuals are to live orderly lives.

Two groups of women are mentioned: older and younger. What is Titus to tell them?

> *Older women likewise are to be reverent in their behavior, not malicious gossips, nor enslaved to much wine, teaching what is good, so that they may encourage the young women to love their husbands, to love their children, to be sensible, pure, workers at home, kind, being subject to their own husbands, so that the word of God will not be dishonored.*
> Titus 2:3-5

Encourage The Young Women

As we look for an answer we can make three lists.

What are older women to be instructed to do? (v. 3-4)
- ∼ Be reverent in their behavior
- ∼ Not be malicious gossips
- ∼ Not be enslaved to much wine
- ∼ Teach what is good
- ∼ Encourage the young women

What are they to encourage the young women to do? (v. 4-5)
- ∼ Love their husbands
- ∼ Love their children
- ∼ Be sensible
- ∼ Be pure
- ∼ Be workers at home
- ∼ Be kind
- ∼ Be subject to their own husbands

Why? (v. 5)
- ∼ To honor the word of God

I found it interesting that Paul tells Titus to instruct the older women, but they in turn are to encourage the young women. How are they to do this? By the example of their behavior and with their words.

How many of you have heard (or said), "Do as I say, not as I do?" As a kid I must have heard my mother say that a million times. She was telling me not to follow her example, but her instructions. A pretty common method of leadership, wouldn't you say? In 1 Peter 5:1-3, Peter addresses two types of leadership.

> *Nor yet as lording it over those allotted to your charge, but proving to be examples to the flock.*   1 Peter 5:3

The Women of Titus Chapter 2

One can either lead by bossing folks around, or lead by example. Why is this important? Well, think of another pretty common saying – "Everybody does it." How many times have we heard that! But it makes a point; human nature judges its own actions by what others are doing. Christians however, are not to follow this pattern. Christians are not only to heed the instructions of Scripture, but also to set a godly example for others to follow. Jesus said:

> *If I had not come and spoken to them, they would not have sin, but now they have no excuse for their sin.*   John 15:22

Not only did Jesus instruct them, but He set the example because He did not sin Himself. In other words, the excuse "Everyone else does it" no longer applies. As followers of Christ, we are expected to not sin either, no matter what others are doing. Either way, we set an example.

One of the greatest eye openers I ever experienced happened when my daughter was a preteen. It was Saturday, our usual day for major housecleaning chores. On this particular day, I happened to be gone for most of the morning. When I returned, my daughter had finished all the housework, including the chores I usually did. My husband, who noticed what a good job she had done, complimented her on it. "Well," she replied, "I just did what I thought Mom would do." He told me this as a compliment, but actually it quite shocked me. Although I didn't know it, *she had been observing me and had followed my example when faced with the same task.* What a humbling experience.

This begs the obvious questions then. Who is watching you? Children? Family? Friends? Neighbors? Co-workers? Others? For whom are you setting an example? Like it or not, all of them.

Application? I'd like to encourage you with what I try to keep in mind for myself:

> *Let us consider how to stimulate one another to love and good deeds.*   Heb. 10:24

Whom Do You Admire?

One of the homeschool groups with which we used to be involved was a group called Keepers of the Faith[1]. Mostly this was for my son, who was younger than his sister. Although she was usually willing to help, she sometimes lamented being the only teenager in that group, as all the lessons and activities were geared toward younger children. I explained to her how important her example was to the younger girls. I pointed to the women of Titus chapter 2 and said, "Everyone is older than somebody else."

This wasn't exactly a literal interpretation of the text, because if we read Titus 2:3-5 carefully, we can see certain qualifiers which define the two groups of women. But it does bring up a principle of application, because there is something here to heed: what kind of example do we set, and whose examples are we following?

We all set an example whether we intend to or not. But another question we can ask is this: what examples do we choose to follow? From observing people over the years, it seems to me that we tend to imitate what we admire: in how we dress, in how we act, in what we say, and how we say it.

Whom do you want to be like? Most Christians would probably say Jesus. It's true, His is the example we should all follow, but there can also be indivduals or even peer groups which influence us. So, in the modern world, whom do you admire? Whose advice do you seek? Whom do you try to be like, look like? Is it a real person of your acquaintance? Someone from the sports or entertainment industry? A television character? Your social circle at work, school, or church? Whose leadership are you following?

From the book of Titus, we can get an idea of the kind of person we should be looking to admire.

Encourage The Young Women

> *Older women likewise are to be reverent in their behavior, not malicious gossips, nor enslaved to much wine, teaching what is good, that they may encourage the younger women*
> *Titus 2:3-4a*

From these verses we can make a list of qualities:

- ∼ Reverent behavior
- ∼ No malicious gossip
- ∼ Not enslaved to much wine
- ∼ Teaching what is good
- ∼ Encouraging younger women

Most of these seem pretty straightforward, but we can still take a closer look at each item with word studies and cross references.

Next, I'd like to show you how to do Greek word studies so that we can dig deeper into the original meanings of New Testament words. After that, we'll take a closer look at the qualities of being a good example.

[1]Keepers of the Faith, http://www.keepersofthefaith.com/

How To Do A Word Study

Word studies are one of the things that make Bible study exciting. When we approach the Bible with a deliberate and reasonable process, then word studies are an important part in how we accurately interpret a book or passage. Remember, interpretation asks, "What does it mean?" Word studies help answer that question.

I believe it is fairly common knowledge that the Old Testament was originally written primarily in Hebrew (with some Aramaic), and the New Testament in Koine Greek. Any translation into another language is subject to the translators' interpretation of the meanings of the words and how they are being used. To understand the author's intended meaning, we need to do a word study. This enables us to determine the meaning of the original Hebrew or Greek word. It is from both definition and context that we can better understand what the author wants to say.

<u>TOOLS</u>: Word studies do require tools. The basics are a concordance and a dictionary.

A concordance gives an alphabetical listing of all the words used in the Bible. *Strong's Exhaustive Concordance of the Bible* is probably the most well known, but there are others. Strong's should be available at any Christian bookstore. Also, since it is public domain, it can be found online at numerous Bible study websites. (See "Resources" page 262.)

By dictionary I mean a language dictionary for Greek or Hebrew. While a concordance will give a brief definition of a word, a good dictionary will give an expanded definition. In fact, many Greek or Hebrew dictionaries are keyed to Strong's, making it even easier to find the word in question.

Dictionaries that I have used and can recommend include:

Vine's Expository Dictionary of New Testament Words. This dictionary is a classic. Look for an edition that is keyed to Strong's. Available at most Christian bookstores, there are also online versions of Vine's.

The Complete Word Study Dictionary: New Testament by Spiros Zodhiates; 1992, AMG Publishers, Chattanooga, TN. This is the one I use most. Companioned with *The Complete Word Study New Testament,* which features the Greek section of Strong's concordance, it combines quite a few word study tools. It and the following are available from Christian bookstores or online booksellers.

The Complete Word Study Dictionary: Old Testament, 1994. Also from AMG Publishers. This is the companion volume to *The Complete Word Study Old Testament.*

Theological Wordbook of the Old Testament; Harris, Archer, and Waltke; 1980; Moody Press, Chicago. Often abbreviated TWOT, this is two volumes. An index in the back of the second volume keys all Hebrew words to Strong's.

PROCEDURE:

1. Start with your concordance. It is divided into three sections: English, Hebrew, and Greek.

2. In the English section, find the word you want to look up. Strong's uses the King James Version. If you're using Strong's and another version, you will need to find the same word in KJV first.

3. In the middle column, find the scripture reference for the word you're researching.

How To Do A Word Study

Using "likewise" from Titus 2:3 as an example, we find it in the alphabetical English section, and then look for our Scripture reference in the middle column. (In the listings, "likewise" is abbreviated as the letter L.)

```
that ye l read the epistle from............... Col 4:16    3668
L must the deacons be grave, not......... 1Ti 3:8     5615
L also the good works of some are...... 1Ti 5:25    5615
The aged women l, that they be in...... Titus 2:3   5615
Young men l exhort to be sober........... Titus 2:6   5615
he also himself l took part of................ Heb 2:14    3898
L also was not Rahab the harlot .......... Jas 2:25    3668
L, ye wives, be in subjection to ............ 1Pet 3:1    3668
L, ye husbands, dwell with them .......... 1Pet 3:7      36
```

In the right hand column is the Strong's number. You can see from this brief excerpt that there are several different numbers listed for "likewise." This tells us that more than one Greek word was translated thus.

4. Note the Strong's number and turn to the Greek dictionary in the back.

5. Look up that number in the dictionary.

```
an exclamation of adoration:—hosanna.

5615. ὡσαύτως hōsautōs, ho-sow'-toce; from
5613 and an adv. from 846; as thus, i.e. in the same
way:—even so, likewise, after the same (in like)
manner.

5616. ὡσεί hōsei, ho-sī'; from 5613 and 1487; as
```

Here is "likewise," found in the Greek section of Strong's. Note that it gives us:
a) The Greek word, the English transliteration (Greek characters translated into equivalent English ones), and the pronunciation.

b) "from" tells us something about the origin of the word.
c) A brief definition is in italics.
d) After the colon followed by a dash (:—) are other ways in which the same Greek word has been translated in the KJV.

TROUBLESHOOTING — If the definition makes absolutely no sense, check to make sure you are in the correct section (Greek or Hebrew)!

6. For an expanded definition, use your Vine's or other dictionary. Most of them are coded to Strong's numbers, so it is easy to look up the correct word.

That's the basics. Granted, "likewise" isn't a terribly exciting word, but now you can begin to look up words on your own. And with that skill, you can begin to interpret the Bible accurately, on your own.

Who Are The Older Women?

> <u>Older women</u> likewise are to be reverent in their behavior, not malicious gossips, nor enslaved to much wine, teaching what is good, that they may encourage the young women.
> Titus 2:3-4a

We've already taken a look at how we all set an example no matter what our age, but verse three focuses on a particular group - older women. Our first question ought to be, "Who are they?"

In the Greek, we're actually dealing with one word here, πρεσβυτις, transliterated *presbutis* (Strong's #4247). This is the feminine form of *presbutes* which means "old man". Both are from the same root from which we get our terms "presbyters" or "church elders."

Titus is the only place in the New Testament that uses *presbutis* (older or aged women). An argument might be made that it could refer not only to chronological age, but to spiritual maturity. This may be plausible, but if we examine the verses closely, we can pick up other clues as to whom the author is actually referring.

> Older women likewise are to be reverent in their behavior, not malicious gossips, nor enslaved to much wine, teaching what is good, that they may encourage the young women to love their husbands, to love their children, to be sensible, pure, workers at home, kind, being subject to their own husbands.
> Titus 2:3-5

We can note that "young women" are associated with "children" and "workers at home". This doesn't mean that the older women don't have children and housework. After all, if they are to teach and encourage the young women in these things, then obviously they have the necessary knowledge and experience. However, we can also note that if the older women have enough time on their hands to waste it drinking and gossiping, then they probably don't have young children around with all the extra housework that entails!

From the text itself we can see that we are looking at exactly what it says - two generations of women.

This seems pretty straightforward, so is there anything about "older women" that we can apply to our own lives? For those of us who are empty nesters, we see in these verses a pattern for the way we are to live our lives as mature Christian women. We are not to waste our time on fruitless pursuits, but are to set an example for the younger women by our behavior, attitudes, and words. Young women, you might assume that this doesn't apply to you yet, but consider this: one day you too will be an older woman. Are you on that path to Christian maturity which will qualify you to be an example and teacher to others?

In the next chapter we'll start to look at the characteristics of spiritual maturity which older women are supposed to display.

Older Women Likewise: Women in Christian Leadership

Leadership / Followship. There have been some Christian groups which I have declined to join because I didn't care to follow in the direction they were going. This is true not only for myself, but also of the groups and activities I chose for my children. On the other hand, when I found myself in leadership positions, I had to consider in what direction I was leading. As women, there are some things we need to consider here. How do we know if we are qualified for leadership? How do we evaluate someone else's qualifications for leadership? With whom should we align ourselves? How do we know whose advice to take? How do we know whose example to follow when we are uncertain of our own circumstances? The book of Titus offers answers.

> Older women <u>likewise</u> are to be reverent in their behavior, not malicious gossips, nor enslaved to much wine, teaching what is good, that they may encourage the young women.
> Titus 2:3-4a

In reading those verses, I notice two things. First, there is a list of qualities to consider. Secondly, I notice the word "likewise." Do you remember that this word was the example I used in "How To Do A Word Study"? It doesn't seem like a very meaty word to study, but its being there points to something else. It points to what went before.

> Likewise. Strong's 5615, ωσανυτως, *hosautos* - in the same way. Zodhiates[1] adds, "In the same or like manner."

The question then is, "In the same way as what?" To answer that, we need to look at the preceding verse.

Encourage The Young Women

Older men are to be temperate, dignified, sensible, sound in faith, in love, in perseverance.   Titus 2:2

From "likewise" then, we can see that these same qualities are to apply to the women in verse three. They too are to be temperate, dignified, sensible, sound in faith, sound in love, sound in perseverance.

From both verses, we have a more complete list of the qualities of spiritual maturity for women.

~ Temperate
~ Dignified
~ Sensible
~ Sound in faith
~ Sound in love
~ Sound in perseverance
~ Reverent
~ Not malicious gossips
~ Not enslaved to much wine
~ Teach what is good

I think it is important to point out that even though we are dealing with older women in verses three and four, biological age doesn't necessarily correlate with maturity. An older person can be exceptionally immature, and a younger person can be exceptionally mature. It's a matter of attitude and behavior, which manifest themselves in what we say and how we say it, and what we do and how we do it. Either way, we set an example whether we intend to or not. Because of this, spiritual maturity should be one of the most important qualifications for Christian leadership.

---

[1] Spiros Zodhiates, *The Complete Word Study Dictionary: New Testament* (Chattanooga, AMG Publishers, 1992) 1503

Temperance: For Drunks Only?

I'd like to spend a little time taking a closer look at the qualities of a spiritually mature woman. The first quality on the list is temperance.

It's a rather old fashioned word, evoking images of the Temperance Movement of the 1800s and Prohibition of the 1920s, of speakeasies and bootleg liquor. Not a word we consider much today. Yet it is one of the qualities of spiritual maturity listed in Titus chapter two. Setting aside it's historical usage and connotations, our question should be, "What does the Bible mean when it says to be temperate?"

> Temperate. Strong's #3524, νηφαλεος (or νηφαλιος), *nephaleos* (or *nephalios*) - sober, circumspect in a figurative sense, vigilant. Zodhiates expands the definition: "sober, temperate, self-controlled, especially in respect to wine. Used metaphorically meaning sober-minded, watchful, circumspect ... that state of mind which is free from the excessive influence of passion, lust, or emotion."[1]

In reading over the definition, we can begin to understand why different translations often seem to say different things. It goes back to how the translator chose to translate a particular word. This is why word studies are necessary. For this study, I am using the New American Standard Bible, although I also refer to the King James Version because many of the study tools reference that.

Now that we have a basic definition of *nephaleos*, we can get a better understanding of its meaning by taking a look at how it is used elsewhere in the New Testament. One way to do this would be by looking for the same Greek word in Strong's. That, however, will not tell us where *nephaleos* is used when translated into a different English word. Several online tools can help us find where it is used, but I like *The New Englishman's Greek Concordance and Lexicon*. This book lists all Greek words by its Strong's number. Under each entry, it lists all the verses in the New Testament in which each Greek word is used regardless of how it is translated. It is here that we see that *nephaleos* occurs three times.

Let's take a look at these verses and apply some of our observation techniques.

> *An overseer then, must be above reproach, the husband of one wife, <u>temperate</u>, prudent, respectable, hospitable, able to teach, not addicted to wine or pugnacious, but gentle, uncontentious, free from the love of money.*
>
> 1 Timothy 3:2-3

Who are the author and recipient? Paul to Timothy
Who is the subject of the verses? Overseers
Why? Paul is giving Timothy a list of qualifications for the office of overseer.
How is "temperate" being used? As one of the character traits in that list.

> *Women must likewise be dignified, not malicious gossips, but <u>temperate</u>, faithful in all things.*
>
> 1 Timothy 3:11

Who are the author and recipient? Paul to Timothy
About *whom* is Paul writing? Women.
Why? Paul is giving Timothy a list of qualifications for women associated with deacons.
How is "temperate" being used? It is listed as a character trait.

Temperance: For Drunks Only?

Older men are to be <u>temperate</u>, dignified, sensible, sound in faith, in love, in perseverance.

Titus 2:2

Who are the author and recipient? Paul to Titus
Who is the subject? Older men
Why? That the church in Crete might be set in order (1:5)
How is "temperate" used? As a quality of orderly behavior.

What conclusions can we draw? From these usages of the word, we can see that temperance is a quality of inner character. It is not something to be imposed on us by rules and laws, as was the case with the Temperance Movement. In fact, we may well ask if temperance applies only to drinking alcohol. From the text and the definition, I say no.

Why do I say that? First, because "not addicted to wine" (1 Tim. 2:3) and "nor enslaved to much wine" (Titus 2:3) are listed in addition to temperance. Second, from the definition. Certainly temperance can apply to drinking alcohol, but the definition is much broader than that. As Zodhiates points out, it implies not being controlled by our own passions, lusts, or emotions; it implies self-control.

Note that the definitions of temperance and supporting verses address our character, or inner Self. This is important because if we can control our impulses and emotions, then we can control our behavior.

The question for us, then, is do we control our emotions and desires, or do they control us? The desire for alcohol is one example, as are drugs and other addictive substances. But what else? What other desires and passions might need self-control? How about emotional temperance to control outbursts of anger? What about self-control in regards to food and eating? What about the type of entertainment we like? Or our language; the words and phrases we use. Do they dictate what we do and say, or do we need to learn to control them?

If we want to grow in spiritual maturity and Christlikeness, then temperance is needed in any area of life that can distract us from being spiritually, mentally, and emotionally alert, or from being self-controlled in our behavior, thoughts, and feelings. An easy task? Not at all. But it's up to each one of us to take our own inner inventory, and then choose whether or not to strive for temperance in our lives.

---

[1]Spiros Zodhiates, *The Complete Word Study Dictionary: New Testament* (Chattanooga, AMG Publishers, 1992) 1010

Dignity: A Basic Human Right?

As I prepared to write this, I contemplated the word "dignity." In trying to understand it as a character trait of a spiritually mature Christian, I thought about how it is commonly used today. Mostly it is seems to be used in association with medical care of the terminally ill, but in poking around the internet, I found it popping up in discussions on bioethics (for example, cloning or stem cell research). In health care, dignity is presented as a basic human right. In terms of bioethics, the discussions I read seem to focus on how to define the word in such a way as to defend one's own point of view.

On another level, when used as descriptive word, "dignified" seems to carry a connotation of formality in the sense of stuffiness, as in "stuffed shirt" or "old fogy." In that sense, dignity does not exactly have a positive connotation in our casual American society and is certainly not appealing to today's youth.

For our purposes, however, we want to set aside common ideas about the meaning of a word. As we look at Christian maturity in Titus 2:2, we need to let the Bible define the word, not society, whose usage and meanings of words are constantly changing with the times.

It is from the biblical definition that we can ask, "What difference does it make in my own life?" To answer this, we need to look at dignity on a practical level, not a philosophical one. We need to understand that biblically, it is not a matter of rights, but of character.

Dignity is the second item on our list in Titus 2:2-3.

Older men are to be temperate, <u>dignified</u>, sensible, sound in faith, in love, in perseverance. Older women likewise.
Titus 2:2-3a

Let's take a look at it.

> Dignified. Strong's #4586, in the Greek, σεμνος, transliterated *semnos* - venerable, honorable. In the KJV it is translated as "grave" or "honest." Of *semnos* Vine[1] says, "Cremer describes it as denoting what inspires reverence and awe.... The word points to seriousness of purpose and to self-respect in conduct."

Self-respect. What an excellent term. In *The New Englishman's Greek Concordance and Lexicon*, we can note that *semnos* is defined as "honorable, worthy of respect."[2] We can also note that it occurs four times in the Greek New Testament. Besides the verse we're studying in Titus chapter two, we find it in two verses in 1 Timothy.

> *Deacons likewise must be men of <u>dignity</u>, not double-tongued, or addicted to much wine, or fond of sordid gain.*
> 1 Tim. 3:8

> *Women must likewise be <u>dignified</u>, not malicious gossips, but temperate, faithful in all things.*
> 1 Tim. 3:11

From these plus our verse in Titus, we see dignity as a character trait of spiritual maturity.

The last reference is found in a different sort of list:

> *Finally brethren, whatever is true, whatever is <u>honorable</u>, whatever is right, whatever is pure, whatever is lovely, whatever is of good repute, if there is any excellence and if anything worthy of praise, let your mind dwell on these things.*
> Phil. 4:8

Dignity: A Basic Human Right?

In this passage Paul is instructing the believers in Philippi in how to have the peace of God. *Semnos* here is translated as "honorable," and is part of a checklist for guarding our thoughts.

How do we incorporate biblical dignity into own lives? I think Vine's term, "self-respect in conduct" is a good starting place. It forces us to examine our actions. We sometimes like to pat ourselves on the back for things we do, but other times we hope no one notices. What helps me is to think about the things I need to do, or am tempted to do, before I do them. I try to ask myself, "What would I do if I knew others were watching? Would they see my actions as admirable?" Then I remind myself that God is always watching. He is the perpetual audience to my life: in the things I do, the things I say, the things I think.

Biblical dignity then, is not something granted to us; it is something that we work toward.

---

[1] W. E. Vine, Merrill F. Unger, William White, Jr., *Vine's Expository Dictionary of Biblical Words* (Thomas Nelson Publishers, NY, 1985) 278

[2] Wigram-Green, *The New Englishman's Greek Concordance and Lexicon* (Hendrickson, Peabody, MA, 1982) 782

Being Sensible

"Sensible" is another word that shows up on several lists in the New Testament - four, in fact. These are always lists of character traits for various groups of people. Of the four times it is used, two of them are in the second chapter of Titus.

> Older men are to be temperate, dignified, <u>sensible</u>, sound in faith, in love, in perseverance.　　　　　　　　Titus 2:2

> [Young women (v 4)] are to be <u>sensible</u>, pure, workers at home, kind, being subject to their own husbands, that the word of God may not be dishonored.　　　　Titus 2:5

> An overseer, then, must be above reproach, the husband of one wife, temperate, <u>prudent</u>, respectable, hospitable, able to teach.
> 　　　　　　　　　　　　　　　　　　　　1 Tim. 3:2

> [For the overseer must be (v 7)] hospitable, loving what is good, <u>sensible</u>, just, devout, self-controlled.　　Titus 1:8

> Sensible. Strong's #4998, σωφρων, *sophron* - safe, sound in mind, i.e. self-controlled (moderate as to opinion or passion). KJV translates *sophron* as discreet, sober, or temperate. Zodhiates[1] explains further; "self-disciplined in one's freedom, self-restrained in all passions and desires."

My first thought in reading this definition is that it is very similar to the "temperance" (*nephaleos*) of Titus 2:2. In fact, the term "self-controlled" is used in both definitions. What the NASB translates "temperate," the KJV translates as "sober." What the KJV translates as "temperate," the

NASB translates as "sensible." Both words use the same terms in their definitions: sober, self-controlled, temperate.

This seems a bit confusing, so I decide to do some cross referencing. As the next step in doing word studies, cross references show how a particular word is used in Scripture. This can shed light on its meaning. I use my Strong's concordance to find them. When I look up the English word, I find all the listings in Scripture for that particular word. The Strong's numbers give me the clue as to the original Greek word I might be looking for. In the case of *sophron* (#4998), however, it isn't particularly helpful since both *sophron* and *nephaleos* are being used in the same context: in lists describing spiritual maturity.

My next thought is to look for a clue in the roots of the two words. I can also do this with my Strong's concordance. I find that the root of *nephaleos* (temperance) means self-control specifically in regards to wine, although in Titus 2, Paul used it in a much broader sense. *Sophron* (sensible) comes from two root words: one meaning sound, one meaning understanding. Putting those two together would enable us to interpret it to mean "of sound understanding".

Does all this seem to be putting too fine a point on it? Maybe so, but I think that Paul is pointing out that there are two areas in our lives which need self-control. The first is from things which can impair our ability to think and act rationally. This can definitely be from wine, which must have been a problem in the first century. But I think for us, it can include other addictive substances; beer or liquor, drugs, tobacco, gambling, etc. Anything which dominates our lives because we have no control over them. They control us. They can become our masters instead of the Lord, so that they come first rather than Him. Our service to the Lord is severely impaired because we have no self-control.

Being Sensible

The second area of self-control is to keep from reacting impulsively to people and situations, without thinking through the consequences of our words and actions. We usually do this when we assume we know what's going on, or when our emotions are in control. As Paul told the Corinthians:

> *We are destroying speculations and every lofty thing raised up against the knowledge of God, and we are taking every thought captive to the obedience of Christ.* 2 Cor. 10:5

This prevents the proverbial putting of one's foot in one's mouth! Paul tells Titus that mature Christians are not to be this way. They are to be in control of what they say and do. They are to be sound in mind or sensible.

Time for reflection. How does this apply to me?

∼ Am I sensible?

∼ Do I have sound judgment?

∼ Do I have self-control in my thought life and over my impulses?

∼ Do I react without thinking?

∼ Do I let my assumptions make decisions for me?

Definitely some food for thought and an object for prayer.

---

[1] Spiros Zodhiates, *The Complete Word Study Dictionary: New Testament* (Chattanooga, AMG Publishers, 1992) 1363

Spiritual Soundness

"...be...<u>sound</u> in faith, in love, in perseverance." Titus 2:2

What does that word "sound" mean to you? In the above context, I mean. Does it seem like an important Bible word? It's not a word I would ordinarily think to research, but here, it is being used in reference to three words that are very important in Christian teaching: faith, love, and perseverance.

> Sound. Strong's #5198, ὑγιαινω, hugiaino – to have sound health, i.e. be well (in body). Figuratively, to be uncorrupt or true in doctrine. Also translated in the KJV as whole, wholesome, safe and sound, and be in health.

Obviously in Titus 2:2 it is being used figuratively.

In *The New Englishman's Greek Concordance and Lexicon*, I note that the word *hugiaino* is used twelve times in the New Testament. For this study, I'm not interested in its literal references to health, so I'll just look at the figurative ones. As I examine these verses my questions are, "In what is a Christian to be sound? In what am I to be whole, uncorrupt, and true?"

> And whatever else is contrary to <u>sound teaching.</u> 1 Tim. 1:10

> If anyone advocates a different doctrine and does not agree with <u>sound words</u>.   1 Tim. 6:3

> Retain the standard of <u>sound words</u>.   2 Tim. 1:13

They will not endure <u>sound doctrine</u>. 2 Tim. 4:3

May be able to both exhort in <u>sound doctrine</u>. Titus 1:9

That they may be <u>sound in faith</u>. Titus 1:13

Speak the things which are fitting for <u>sound doctrine</u>.
Titus 1:2

<u>Sound in</u> faith, in love, in perseverance. Titus 2:2

These verses give me a list of things in which a Christian needs to be sound. However, before I can make any conclusions, I need to take a closer look at the words which "sound" is describing. Since this study is focusing on Titus chapter two, I'll take a closer look at faith, love, and perseverance.

Is Faith Blind?

Blind faith - admirable or foolhardy? I admit that I'm not even sure from where the term "blind faith" came. Does it mean a faith so trusting as to leap off a proverbial cliff without knowing where one will land? Does it mean accepting what someone else says about Scripture without researching for oneself? Does it mean an ignorant faith, assuming things without knowledge? Or does it somehow refer to Jesus's healing of the blind? Is it an appropriate way to describe an important tenant of Christianity?

The verse under study here is Titus 2:2, in which older men (and likewise women, v. 3) are told to be "sound in faith." Having already studied the word "sound" and understanding it to mean "whole, true in doctrine," we need to take a look at the word faith next.

> Faith. Strong's #4102, πιστις, *pistis* - persuasion, conviction of religious truth or the truthfulness of God, especially reliance upon Christ for salvation; abstractly, constancy in such a profession; by extension, the system of religious truth itself.

It is used 244 times in the New Testament. In one of them, the Bible offers its own definition:

> Now <u>faith</u> is the assurance of things hoped for, the conviction (evidence) of things not seen.   Hebrews 11:1

What does it mean, then, to be "sound in faith"? By combining our two definitions, it could be said that it means to have an assurance or conviction based on whole, accurate doctrine or teaching, not only on that for which we have empirical, visible proof.

Going back to our original question (is faith blind?), we can now say that a sound faith is not a blind faith. Sound faith is a confidence based on the full knowledge of something. Even so, does this mean that faith is simply a matter of accepting that knowledge as true?

As Christians, we know that certain knowledge is required for salvation:

- ∼ I must understand that I have sin. I am disobedient to God and there is an eternal consequence for this - death. Death is the penalty for sin which must be paid.
- ∼ I must know that I can never pay that penalty on my own. Because of this, God Himself became a man, took my place, and willingly accepted the death penalty for my sin.
- ∼ I must understand that by doing this, Jesus overcame death forever, and that eternal life is available to everyone who believes.

However, simply knowing all this is not enough.

You believe that God is one. You do well; the demons also believe and shudder.   James 2:19

Knowledge and belief alone are not enough for salvation, I must act on it as well.

1. I must own up to my sin without making excuses. I must utterly reject my sin and turn from it forever (repent), which I do by confessing it and asking God's forgiveness.
2. I must accept what Jesus did for me by dying on the cross, and I must receive His free gift of eternal life.

Is Faith Blind?

Those actions then, are what require the kind faith of which we're talking.

So then. Are you good to go in this department? Been there, done that, got the t-shirt? Checked that box and ready to get on with life? In other words, is salvation all there is to being sound in faith? If it isn't, what else is there?

Faith is an Action Word

About 27 years ago, I heard Dr. Tony Evans preach at Second Baptist Church in Houston, TX. He made a statement about faith that made quite an impression on me. He said that the opposite of faith is not doubt; the opposite of faith is disobedience. As we've seen through word studies, faith is defined as more than simple belief; rather, it is an accurate knowledge of which we are so convinced that it makes a difference in our lives.

For the Christian, faith begins with repentance and salvation. When I look around, however, I see too many Christians for whom salvation doesn't seem to make a difference. On occasion I ask some of them about their relationship with the Lord. They know that Jesus died for their sins and that now they are going to heaven. God's will for their lives is to go to church and try to do good. But too often they don't live any differently than the unsaved, and the evidence of their Christianity focuses only on a particular point in time - their salvation experience. I have a heavy burden for such as these. The salvation experience isn't supposed to be the pinnacle of our Christian walk; it is supposed to be the beginning.

As Paul said to Agrippa,

> *They should repent and turn to God, performing deeds appropriate to repentance.*   Acts 26:20

That is biblical faith. The book of James speaks much on this. For example,

> *What use is it, my brethren, if a man says he has faith but he has no works? Can that faith save him?*   James 2:14

We might well ask, "If I believe that Jesus is the Son of God who died for my sins, then isn't simply believing that good enough? If salvation is a free gift and works don't get me into heaven, then so what?" However, if we understand that faith is acting on that belief, then we see that James is trying to make a point.

> *You see that a man is justified by works, and not by faith alone.* James 2:24

The point is that our actions prove what we really believe. Let's try to bring this down to a personal level. For example, I recite Phil. 4:19 and say that I believe God will meet all my needs. But -

~ I pray for God to provide something, then run out and use my credit card to get it.
~ My garage is full of things I could donate to the needy but don't, just in case I might need them.
~ When I think my prayers aren't being answered, I get mad at God.
~ I don't tithe because then I won't have enough to pay my bills.

Faith is not just believing that God *can* do something; rather it is trusting Him *before* He does something.

Okay. Let's bring this full circle. We need to understand that faith is not a matter of mental agreement, positive thinking, or opinion. Rather, it is action based on accurate knowledge; it is proof of a life in Christ. I think James said it best:

> *For just as the body without the spirit is dead, so also faith without works is dead.* James 2:26

Love: More Than a Feeling?

Older men are to be temperate, dignified, sensible, sound in faith, in <u>love</u>, in perseverance. Older women likewise...
Titus 2:2-3a

Choose the correct answer. In the above verses love means:
1. help and serve others through good works
2. be friendly and try to like everybody
3. continue to be sexually active in old age
4. put family first

The answer one chooses will depend upon how one interprets "love." Any one of them could be correct because all of these possible answers are taken from the four Greek words for love: *agape* (sacrificial, unconditional love), *philia* (affection amongst friends), *eros* (physical attraction and passion), and *storge* (love of family). To know which meaning Paul intended I need to know what word was used in the original Greek text. [Hint: only *agape* and *philia* are used in the New Testament.] That means I'll have to roll up my sleeves, pull out my Strong's Concordance, and do a word study.

> Love, Strong's #26, αγαπη, *agape* - affection or benevolence. Rendered charity in the KJV. Used 116 times in the New Testament. Zodhiates[1] expands that definition, saying "It is God's willful direction toward man. It involves God doing what He knows is best for man and not necessarily what man desires." And from Vine[2] "Christian love... is not an impulse from the feelings, it does not always run with the natural inclinations, nor does it spend itself only upon those for whom some affinity is discovered. Love seeks the

welfare of all and works no ill to any, love seeks the opportunity to do good."

As Christians, we can best understand *agape* in the sense of John 3:16; God loving the world enough to sacrifice His beloved Son for it. However, it is difficult to understand *agape* in terms of human application, because it is hard for us to separate the concept of love from feeling and emotion. In looking at the Lord's sacrifice for us, we see in Mark 14:36 that as willing as He was, Jesus didn't feel like dying on the cross. As with faith, we need to understand that *love is an action based on obedience to God's word rather than on our feelings.*

But how do we do something that seems so contrary to human nature? 1 Corinthians 13:4-8a offers practical advice:

> *Love is patient, love is kind, and is not jealous; love does not brag and is not arrogant, does not act unbecomingly; it does not seek its own, is not provoked, does not take into account a wrong suffered, does not rejoice in unrighteousness, but rejoices with the truth; bears all things, believes all things, hopes all things, endures all things. Love never fails.*
>
> 1 Cor. 13:4-8a

These actions are choices we can make regardless of how we feel. For example, I can choose to be patient with another person. I can choose to be kind. I can choose to not elevate myself by bragging about how important or accomplished I am. I can choose to not keep track of how many times they've offended me. I can choose to not gloat over their misfortunes. I can choose to not let them get my goat. In other words, these are things I can do no matter how I feel.

Love: More Than a Feeling?

Easy? No way! But then, whoever said Christianity was for wimps? Success all boils down to who's in control - you or your emotions?

But what if the person doesn't deserve my *agape*? The answer to this points back to faith, i.e., a willingness to trust God enough to be obedient to His Word whether the recipient of my service and sacrifice deserves it or not. It means literally following Jesus' example.

The bottom line? Soundness in love is proof of our Christianity. It proves that we are followers of the Lord Jesus Christ. He said it Himself.

> *A new commandment I give to you, that you love one another, even as I have loved you, that you also love one another. By this all men will know that you are My disciples, if you have love for one another.*
>
> John 13:34-35

---

[1] Spiros Zodhiates, *The Complete Word Study Dictionary: New Testament* (AMG Publishers, Chattanooga, 1992) 66

[2] W .E. Vine, Merrill F. Unger, and William White, Jr., *Vine's Expository Dictionary of Biblical Words,* (Thomas Nelson Publishers, New York, 1985) 382

Circumstances Getting You Down?

My sister-in-law was a parent's nightmare. She smoked, she drank, she did drugs, she ran around all hours of the night, she dropped out of high school. She restlessly flitted from job to job, preferring to live off her mother and stay home to watch cartoons all day. She did this well into her 30s. Needless to say, she wasn't happy with her life.

She came to me one day and told me that she saw something different about me, and it was something she wanted for herself. I wasted no time in sharing the gospel and leading her in the sinner's prayer. She received it all with great expectation. I was elated.

For a few weeks, she poured over the Bible I had given her. She prayed with me, she went to church, she didn't see her old friends anymore. Then suddenly she dropped it all and went back to her old lifestyle. Worried, I went to her about this and we talked. What I finally realized was that *she hadn't been looking to be saved from her sins, she was looking to be saved from her circumstances.* When God didn't "fix" her circumstances, she figured that religion didn't "work".

Have you ever wanted God to change your circumstances? Or perhaps tried to change them yourself? Do they ever get you down? Have they ever become burdensome to the point where you don't think you can bear them anymore?

This is the next point to address in Titus 2:2.

> Older men are to be temperate, dignified, sensible, sound in faith, in love, in <u>perseverance</u>.   Titus 2:2

We've been looking at the qualities of spiritual maturity listed in that verse. So far I've covered being temperate, dignified, sensible, sound in faith, and sound in love. In the context of that verse alone, these qualities are being applied to older men. Verse 3, however, tells us

> *Older women likewise...*   Titus 2:3a

Even so, I think all of these qualities are relevant to every Christian. Spiritual maturity should be both a personal goal, as well as something in which we train our children. So let's take a look at perseverance.

> Perseverance, Strong's #5281, ὑπομονη, *hupomone* - hopeful endurance, consistency. KJV renders it as "patience." NASB offers an alternate translation of "steadfastness." Zodhiates[1] explains it best; "A bearing up under, patience, endurance as to things or circumstances. This is in contrast to *makrothumia* (Strong's #3115), long-suffering or endurance toward people. *Huponome* is associated with hope (1 Thes 1:3) and refers to that quality of character which does not allow one to surrender to circumstances or succumb under trial."

A mature Christian should view his or her situation with hope and not allow their circumstances to get them down. But how? It's one thing to read and understand what a particular Scripture is telling us to do, but it's often difficult to know how to do it.

I think two things might be helpful here. The first is understanding why God allows us to experience difficult or unpleasant circumstances in the first place. The second is faith. We'll look at those next.

---

[1]Spiros Zodhiates, *The Complete Word Study Dictionary: New Testament* (Chattanooga, AMG Publishers, 1992) 1425

Why Me? Persevering Through Difficulties

When we looked at the word "perseverance" in Titus 2:2, we saw that it referred to a hopeful endurance that does not give up despite trials and circumstances. That brought up the question, "Why does God allow difficulties in the lives of Believers in the first place?"

To answer that question, let's go back to the book of James, which has been a helpful commentary for Titus 2:2.

> Consider it all joy, my brethren, when you encounter various trials, knowing that the testing of your faith produces endurance (perseverance). And let endurance (perseverance) have its perfect result, that you may be perfect (mature) and complete, lacking in nothing. James 1:2-4

In other words, we experience difficult things in life because we are being trained in spiritual maturity. Consider the following verses:

> For whom He foreknew, He also predestined to become conformed to the image of His Son. Romans 8:29

> But speaking the truth in love, we are to grow up in all aspects into Him, who is the head, even Christ. Eph. 4:15

Scripture tells us that the answer to this chapter title question ("Why Me?") is that He wants us to become like Jesus: in words, actions, attitudes, thoughts, and the way we respond to people and circumstances. Many times I've wished that God would do this miraculously so that, "poof," I was automatically Christlike. Unfortunately, that isn't the case. As Paul told the Philippians,

For I am confident of this very thing, that He who began a good work in you will perfect it until the day of Christ Jesus.
Phil. 1:6

That good work is conforming us to the image of Jesus, and it is ongoing until the day of Christ. For whatever reason, God chooses to do this in a practical way, through life experiences.

Sometimes those life experiences are humanly impossible to understand: death, divorce, disease, flood, famine, fire, hurricanes, accidents, unemployment, etc. But does that mean that bad things are God's will? If God is love, why would He allow them to happen at all?

It was never God's will for Mankind to sin in the first place. He forewarned there would be consequences (Gen. 2:16-17), but that didn't stop us. Now, because of sin, we live in a fallen world which operates out of God's original plan. Our difficulties in life result from living in that fallen world. Fortunately, this world as we know it will not last forever (Rev. 21:1). But until time runs its course, God uses these difficulties to prepare us for our eternal life in Christ.

Now, it's one thing to understand this intellectually, but actually walking through tough situations is very difficult, if not impossible. It requires faith. Remember, faith is trusting God enough to be obedient to His Word no matter what is going on in our lives. It doesn't give up when God doesn't immediately change our circumstances, nor does it become angry with God and blame Him for what's going on. Rather, faith clings to His Word in hope, trusting that He is bringing about a greater good in us.

I wish I could say that this is easy, but from experience I know it's not. The best way I know how is to hang on to His Word. I'd like to close by sharing the verses I have clung to during my worst trials. Sometimes all I could do was to repeat them over and over and over.

Why Me? Persevering Through Difficulties

Humble yourselves, therefore, under the mighty hand of God, that He may exalt you at the proper time, casting all your anxiety upon Him because He cares for you. Be of sober spirit, be on the alert. Your adversary, the devil, prowls about like a roaring lion, seeking someone to devour. But resist him, firm in your faith, knowing that the same experiences of suffering are being accomplished by your brethren who are in the world. And after you have suffered for a little while, the God of all grace, who called you to His eternal glory in Christ, will Himself perfect, confirm, strengthen, and establish you. To Him be dominion forever and ever. Amen.

I Peter 5:6-11

Behavior Check for Women in Christian Leadership

Titus 2:2 gave us a description of Christian maturity. Although specifically referring to older men in that verse, it applies to women as well. We know this by virtue of that little word "likewise" in the following verse. Next, I want to start taking a look at that verse.

> Older women likewise, are to be reverent in their behavior, not malicious gossips, nor enslaved to much wine, teaching what is good that they may encourage the young women.
> Titus 2:3-4a

First, let's observe the passage.

Who is being discussed? Older women.
What is the first thing they are to do? Be reverent in their behavior.
Why? That they may teach and encourage the young women.

Next, let's do a couple of word studies.

> Reverent, Strong's #2412, ἱεροπρεπης, *hieroprepes* - reverent, rendered in KJV as "as becometh holiness." Vines[1] explains further, "suited to a sacred character, that which is befitting persons, actions, or things consecrated to God." Titus 2:3 is the only time this word is used in the New Testament.
>
> Behavior, Strong's #2688, καταστημα, *katastema* - a position or condition, demeanor. As with reverent, this is the only time it is used in the New Testament.

Putting the two together, reverent behavior doesn't mean random acts of deference. It doesn't mean being a doormat. It doesn't mean behaving as though inferior to others. Rather, it refers to a manner of life which reflects one's total dedication to God.

This is especially significant because of the leadership role that the older women are to assume as teachers and encouragers. A Christian leader's life should be observably consecrated to God in attitude, outward actions, and demeanor. Why? Because biblical leadership is by example.

> Nor yet as lording it over those allotted to your charge, but proving to be examples to the flock.   1 Peter 5:3

Christian leadership is not telling others what to do and how to do it. It is *showing* others these things. Christian leaders are role models. Christian leadership begins with a life consecrated to God. The responsibility and accountability for this is great:

> Let not many of you become teachers, my brethren, knowing that as such we shall incur a stricter judgment.   James 3:1

Knowing then, that we will be held accountable for how our lives influence others, I'd like to close with some questions for self-reflection:

∼ Is my life 100% set apart to God and for His service?

∼ Do I act like it?

Behavior Check for Women in Christian Leadership

∼ Does it show in my attitude?

∼ Does it show in my speech?

∼ Is there anything in my life that I am keeping for myself?

∼ Is there anything I wouldn't want my pastor to catch me doing or saying?

∼ What things in my life would I not want others to imitate?

It's not that we are perfect in these things, but that we are striving to achieve them though prayer and study of God's Word, taking comfort in the fact that the Lord knows the sincerity of our hearts.

---

[1] W.E. Vine, Merrill F. Unger, and William White, Jr., *Vine's Expository Dictionary of Biblical Words* (Thomas Nelson Publishers, NY, 1985) 55

How Many Kinds of Gossip Are There, Anyway?

> *Older women likewise, are to be reverent in their behavior, <u>not malicious gossips</u>.*   Titus 2:3

Hmmm, at face value it would almost seem as though this is saying that it's okay to gossip as long as it's not malicious. Common sense should tell us this conclusion somehow isn't right! This phrase, "not malicious gossips" certainly demands a closer look.

This is one of those times when looking up the Greek is especially helpful, because we see that "malicious gossips" ("false accusers" in KJV) is actually one word in Koine Greek. I discovered this from my Strong's Concordance. Strong's references the King James translation, so I looked up both false and accuser, and discovered the same reference number for both.

> Malicious gossips. Strong's #1228, διαβολος, *diabolos* - a traducer, specifically Satan. Translated as false accuser, devil, or slanderer in the KJV.

Oh my. I don't know what a traducer is, but the reference to Satan is worrisome.

Zodhiates, in *The Complete Word Study Dictionary: New Testament*, dedicates over three pages to this word's usage in the New Testament. Of its use in Titus 2:3, he says "one who falsely accuses and divides people without any reason... a slanderer."[1]

I was still curious about traducer though. It's not a word in common usage today, so I turned to the 1828 edition of Noah Webster's *American Dictionary of the English Language*. I looked up two words, "gossip" and "traducer".

Gossip was interesting and had several definitions. It could mean a baptismal sponsor or godparent, a tippling companion, one who runs about tattling or telling news, a friend or neighbor, or one who participates in idle talk. This might explain the need for the qualifying "malicious," although the meaning of the word has narrowed over the years.

I also look up traducer, and discovered that it means slanderer or calumniator ("one who falsely and knowingly accuses another of a crime or offense, or maliciously propagates false accusations or reports.")

I think almost all of us will read that definition and think "Gosh, I would never do that!" Still, in our day-to-day relationships, we have to admit that it is easy to become irritated or frustrated with some individuals. If the problem is ongoing, there is a temptation to "warn" others about that person. Or worse, make the problem a "prayer request," being sure to give all the specific details so that everyone will know exactly what to pray about. But is that "doing unto others" (Matt. 7:12)?

The verse that comes to mind for a situation like this is from the book of First Peter,

> *Above all, keep fervent in your love for one another, because love covers a multitude of sins.*   1 Peter 4:10

In other words, love does not expose the sins of others, but keeps them private, trusting God to bring about His perfecting work in their life as well as my own. My public prayer requests should focus on my need for grace in handling the situation, not on the other person's faults or offenses.

What we see here is an application of the *agape* love we studied in "Love: More Than a Feeling?" It must have been a

How Many Kinds of Gossip Are There, Anyway?

problem among women at that time, or Paul wouldn't have addressed it. The question is, is it still a problem in the church today?

---

[1] Spiros Zodhiates, *The Complete Word Study Dictionary: New Testament* (AMG Publishers, Chattanooga, 1992) 419

Nor Enslaved To Much Wine

How you react to the title of this post will largely depend upon your cultural background and denominational persuasion.

> Older women likewise are to be reverent in their behavior, not malicious gossips, <u>nor enslaved to much wine</u>, teaching what is good.   Titus 2:3

Some denominations are staunchly against drinking alcohol in any form, others not so much. Having grown up with an alcoholic mother, I know all too well the devastating consequences of alcohol addiction. However, I'm not going to debate drinking as a moral issue; rather, I want to take a closer look at what Paul meant when he wrote these words to Titus.

The Complete Word Study New Testament is a fairly thick volume which gives the Strong's reference number above each word in the text. In reading Titus 2:3, I see that there are four Greek words to look up:

- Nor (not – KJV). Strong's #3361, μη, *me* - qualified negation, not, nothing, without.

- Enslaved (given – KJV). Strong's #1402, δουλοω, *douloo* - bring into or be under bondage, become or make a servant.

- Much. Strong's #4183, πολυς, *polus* - much, many, often, mostly, largely.

- Wine. Strong's #3631, οινος, *oinos* - wine, literally or figuratively

I have heard a number of fiery, if not elaborate, sermons on the subject of drinking. Most of them focused on the definition of wine and the consequences of drunkenness. Based on my own childhood experience of alcoholism in the family, I could sit there and give the nod of agreement. Even so, the teaching that struck the greatest chord was one I saw on television.

It was many years ago, so I don't recall much of it, but Pat Robertson was teaching on the subject of addiction. He went back to Genesis 1:28, pointing out that Mankind was intended to have dominion over creation. With an addiction, creation has dominion over Man. This is out of order and was never God's perfect plan for His creation.

It was at this point that I realized that drinking, smoking, pill popping, etc., are not a matter of "do's & dont's," but rather a matter of fulfilling the purpose for which we were designed. Alcohol is a physically addictive substance; it can become anyone's master. Therein lies the danger. The alcoholic is no longer free to make his or her own choices, everything revolves around getting the next drink.

I've already addressed addiction in a broader sense ("Temperance: For Drunks Only?"), but Paul specifically mentions wine in Titus 2:3. Obviously this was a problem in his day. It continues to be a problem in our day too.

In context, he was talking about a character trait rather than the act of drinking. In order to be teachers, older women are to display spiritual maturity and strength of character. This is imperative because their example is what validates their teaching. Their lives are to demonstrate loyalty to one master only, the Lord Jesus Christ.

I'll leave you with this as a closing thought – Are you in a leadership position? Could you say that Titus 2:2-3 describes your character? If not, what needs to be corrected? Do you aspire to leadership? Which of the character traits in Titus 2:2-3 do you need to work on? And remember, we're all working on something!

The Problem With Being Good

I have an issue with the word "good". Why? Because not everyone has the same idea about what it means. As with the word love, it can mean different things to different folks, in different times, and different places.

For example, what does a parent mean when they say that a baby is good? Usually they mean a baby who doesn't cry a lot and sleeps all night.

Or what does a teacher mean when they say a student is good? Isn't that a child who does what they're told and doesn't demand a lot of behavioral correction? A parent on the other hand, is more likely to define their scholar's goodness on the basis of the grades they make.

A boss will say we've done a good job if we've met his or her expectations.

"Good" can also refer to things we like, such as good music or a good meal.

But what about moral goodness? Stop for a minute and answer this next question in your mind before reading further.

What is sin?

Did the word "bad" somehow come to mind (as in the opposite of "good")? I've heard quite a few Sunday School and VBS teachers define sin to children in this way: sin is doing bad things. Of course they are referring to a moral bad and good, but in this day of relativism, defining moral goodness isn't all that easy.

Why? Because there is an idea in our society today that if one can produce a plausible reason for one's actions, then the actions aren't really bad. This is a recurring theme in today's cops-and-robbers style entertainment; the good guys are justified in breaking the law in order to catch the bad guys, or, the bad guys had such horrible childhoods that we mentally excuse their actions.

Even worse, moral relativism has found its way into politics. Take, for example, the issue of abortion. To those who believe that we are uniquely and purposefully created by a loving God in His image, then abortion is evil. But to those who believe that we evolved from nothingness and have no other purpose in life than to create our own happiness, then abortion is good. It all boils down to worldview.

Because of all of the above, we obviously can't assume that the people we talk to will interpret these terms the same way we do. Nor do we want to put our own assumptions on what the Bible says.

Well, it appears I've taken the long way around to taking a look at what the Bible means by "good" in this verse:

> *Older women likewise are to be reverent in their behavior, not malicious gossips, nor enslaved to much wine, <u>teaching what is good</u>.*   Titus 2:3

We'll take a look at "teaching what is good" next.

Teaching What Is Good

In the last chapter we looked at some of the modern day ideas about the word "good." In this chapter we'll look at what the Bible means when Paul tells Titus that older women are to be "teaching what is good" in Titus 2:3.

> Teaching what is good. Strong's #2567, καλοδιδασκαλος, kalodidaskalos - a teacher of the right, a teacher of good things. From kalos (2570), good, and didaskalos (1320), teacher. Used only in Titus 2:3.

From Strong's definition alone we can see that it doesn't mean teaching what is pleasing and likable, it is teaching what is right. Of course, like the word "good," "right and wrong" have also fallen victim to postmodern relativism, so we can't look around us to find the correct definition. We need to do a word study.

> Good. Strong's #2570, καλος, kalos - "Constitutionally good without necessarily being benevolent; expresses beauty as a harmonious completeness, balance, proportion."[1]

In other words, biblical goodness is an inner quality rather than an outward display. This brings to mind the first chapter of Genesis, where God looked at the things He created and declared them good. Creation was good because everything was in perfect balance and complete harmony according to His will.

Titus 2:3 then, is telling us that spiritually mature women are to teach younger women to *be* good, not just to do good. But how does one teach that? By giving them a list of do's and don't's? As Paul explained to Timothy,

> *The goal of our instruction is love from a pure heart and a good conscience and a sincere faith.*   1 Timothy 1:5

Why? Because it is possible to do the right things with the wrong motives. How do we know the difference? Because wrong motives always factor in one's Self. If our motive includes the benefit or convenience of Self, then it isn't pure. It isn't *kalos*.

But again, how does one teach this to others? The only way I know is to take them to God's word and let it speak to their hearts and renew their minds (Rom. 12:2).

> *For the word of God is living and active and sharper than any two-edged sword, and piercing as far as the division of soul and spirit, of both joints and marrow, and able to judge the thoughts and intentions of the heart.*   Hebrews 4:12

This is why it is imperative to study the Bible itself, rather than rely solely on study guides and devotionals. While we might agree with what others have to say, it is only God's Word that has the power to transform and renew our hearts and minds.

I think what we're seeing, then, is that women who aspire to leadership must have a personal knowledge of the Scriptures in order to teach them to others. It is a worthy goal, but one which we must not take lightly. My prayer is that each one of us will take this to heart and study diligently, that we might accurately handle the word of truth (2 Timothy 2:14).

---

[1] Spiros Zodhiates, *The Complete Word Study Dictionary: New Testament* (AMG Publishers, Chattanooga, 1992) 814

How Not to Encourage Your Friends and Family

I am not the sort of person that others would peg as an encourager. I have been told that I speak my mind too often and that I am too blunt when I do so. Not that I am deliberately being critical, but that is how I am sometimes perceived by others. I was first able to identify this in myself almost 30 years ago, when I took a MasterLife[1] discipleship class. It was then that I set about to try to be an encourager rather than a discourager.

From that time onward, I made every effort to look for things on which to compliment others: hair, clothes, family, etc. When they were discouraged, I was always ready with my "things could be worse" speech. I made a conscious effort toward this for several years. After a while, however, I realized that people would usually react in one of two ways. Either I only served to puff up their egos (not a goal of Scripture), or they became suspicious of me, wondering what I wanted (not a goal of mine). Eventually I became discouraged with myself and my efforts.

What I'm trying to get to is Titus 2:4. In verses two and three, we looked at older women as leaders, examining the leadership qualifications one by one. In verses four and five, we will learn in what these women are to lead.

> *That they may <u>encourage (teach</u>, KJV) the young women.*
> *Titus 2:4*

Encourage. Strong's #4994, σωφρονιζω, *sophronizo* - to make of sound mind, i.e. to discipline or correct. Teach to be sober. Zodhiates elaborates, "To discipline, train to think and act soberly, discreetly, and in moderation. To correct, to teach".[2]

Encourage The Young Women

What I see here is that biblical encouragement is not trying to make someone feel better about themselves or their circumstances. It's not warm fuzzies and attaboy speeches. Nor is it simply imparting knowledge by telling others what to do and how to do it. The goal of encouragement is a changed life.

I will be the first one to confess that I don't have a handle on how to do this. In the classes I've taught, I have thought about it frequently. There are two verses of scripture which I have found myself contemplating:

> *Let us consider how to stimulate one another to love and good deeds.*   Heb. 10:24

> *Speaking the truth in love.*   Eph. 4:15a

From these, I have realized that I need to commit everything to prayer, from lesson preparation to class discussion. I especially need to pray for the class participants themselves. I pray that it is not my opinions that will stick to their souls, but only God's truth. In a one-on-one situation, I am learning that I must exhibit respect and a genuine caring for the person with whom I am speaking. I must be sensitive to the promptings of the Holy Spirit and how God would have me encourage her.

Titus 2:4 and 5 lists the things in which older women are to encourage young women, but they are not all easy things:

> *Encourage the young women to love their husbands, to love their children, to be sensible, pure, workers at home, kind, being subject to their own husbands, that the word of God may not be dishonored.*   Titus 2:4-5

How Not to Encourage Your Friends and Family

Some of these are things that human nature is naturally resistant to. Because of that, I think it is imperative that women see their husbands and children as ministry. True, this sort of ministry isn't as glamorous as having a recognized position in the church, but as we will see in these verses, it is something that the Lord Himself has given us. An important part of that ministry is to our children, because Christian mothers are supposed to model biblical womanhood to them, boys as well as girls. This is a very powerful position, because by it, mothers shape the next generation and the way they will impact their world.

---

[1] Avery T. Willis, *Masterlife: Discipleship Training for Leaders* (Originally published by the Sunday School Board of the Southern Baptist Convention, N.p., 1982).

[2] Spiros Zodhiates, *The Complete Word Study Dictionary: New Testament* (AMG Publishers, Chattanooga, 1992) 1362

To Love Their Husbands

*W*henever I see the word "love" in the New Testament, I almost always assume it is *agape*. After all, *agape* is the highest form of love; it is the benevolent, sacrificial love which God has toward us and for which Jesus went to the Cross. Besides, *agape* is something every Christian is commanded to do.

So, I was quite surprised when I looked up "love" in this verse

> *That they may encourage the young women <u>to love their husbands</u>.* Titus 2:4a

and discovered it to be something else.

> Love their husbands. Strong's #5362, φιλανδρος, *philandros*, from 5384 (*philos* - fond, friendly) and 435 (*aner* - man, fellow, husband, sir) - fond of man, i.e. affectionate as a wife. Titus 2:4 is the only place it is used in the New Testament.

Ladies, let me ask; how many of you are affectionate toward your husbands? If you're newly married then it probably comes pretty easily. But oftentimes, the longer we are married, the less of a habit it becomes.

Now, I suspect that there are times when being affectionate seems inconvenient, especially when it might lead to something else. And yes, perhaps it might be interpreted as an invitation, especially if the wife is rarely affectionate or the husband has a need to be sexually satisfied. However, sexual passion, *eros*, is not the same thing as *philos*. *Eros* is an important part of marriage, and wives do have a biblical responsibility to sexually satisfy their husbands.

> *Stop depriving one another, except by agreement for a time that you may devote yourselves to prayer and come together again lest Satan tempt you because of your lack of self-control.*
> *I Cor. 7:5*

Philos is something else. Zodhiates helps clarify *philos* for us: "Loved, dear, befriended, friendly, kind ... with the meaning of companion.[1]" This is part of the marital relationship. Why? I believe it is because of God's original design for marriage.

Think about it. What is the purpose of marriage? We are all familiar with the term, "be fruitful and multiply" (Gen. 1:28). But consider this verse:

> *Then the LORD God said, "It is not good for the man to be alone; I will make him a helper suitable for (corresponding to) him."*
> *Gen. 2:18*

Here we see why God created marriage in the first place, for companionship. Let's face it, nobody gets married because they want to be alone. One's marriage partner is to be one's life companion. Affection is the outward manifestation of a special companionship which exists only between husband and wife.

The application question then is, "Do you show a genuine affection toward your husband?" It may come easily for you, but then again, it may not. If it doesn't, why not?

The reasons may be simple or complex. Your answer may very well include, "because he..." Or it may be because you don't feel affection toward him. If you are aware of anger or resentment toward your husband, then affection will be difficult. Those are issues which must definitely be resolved, but remember, godliness isn't based on our feelings. It's based on a decision of will and then choosing to

To Love Their Husbands

act on that decision regardless of feelings. We've already seen this in studying faith and love.

The relationship between husband and wife is to be a reflection of the relationship between Christ and His Church (Eph. 5:31-32). Let us determine that the testimony of our marriages accurately reflects this relationship and attracts others to Christ.

---

[1] Spiros Zodhiates, *The Complete Word Study Dictionary: New Testament* (AMG Publishers, Chattanooga, 1992) 1446

To Love Their Children

After the interesting surprise I received when I researched "To Love Their Husbands," I was eager to get on to the last part of the verse.

> That they may encourage the young women to love their husbands, <u>to love their children</u>.   Titus 2:4

> Love their children. Strong's #5388, φιλοτεκνος, *philoteknos*, from 5384 (*philos* - fond, friendly) and 5043 (*teknon* - one's child, daughter, son) - fond of one's children, i.e. maternal. Used only in Titus 2:4.

I suppose it would seem odd that women should need to be encouraged to be fond of their children. Isn't the maternal bond a natural one?

One would think so. However, anyone who has had the day-in, day-out responsibility of caring for small children knows how exhausting this job can be; physically, mentally, emotionally, and spiritually. I don't know how it was in the 1st century, but in the 21st century we can add society's pressure for women to be part of the workforce, plus feminism's claim that the domestic arts can never be fulfilling. All these things can gradually chip away at any woman's maternal resolve. Then, when we look at the alarming trend of increasing child abuse, neglect, and abandonment, we might well ask, "What has happened to this nation's maternal instincts!"

Very little else is said in the New Testament regarding loving our children. I did find one verse which describes maternal love:

> *But we proved to be gentle among you, as a nursing mother tenderly cares for her own children.* 1 Thes. 2:7

Here, maternal love is used as a comparison, but we can glean two characteristics:

> Gentle. Strong's #2261, ηπιος, *epios* - affable, i.e. mild, kind, gentle.

> Tenderly cares. Strong's #2282, θαλπω, *thalpo* - to brood (as a hen broods her chicks), to foster, to cherish.

Also I found a few other helpful verses. Although addressed to fathers, they nonetheless give us insight into the Lord's heart for raising children:

> *Fathers, do not exasperate your children that they may not lose heart.* Col 3:21

> *And fathers, do not provoke your children to anger, but bring them up in the discipline and instruction of the Lord.*
> Eph 6:4

> Discipline. Strong's #3811, παιδευω, *paideuo* – to train up a child. i.e. educate, chasten (correct), nurture, instruct.

The following verses describe the children of men being considered for church leadership:

> *He must be one who manages his own household well. keeping his children under control with all dignity.*
> 1 Timothy 3:4

To Love Their Children

Namely, if a man be above reproach, the husband of one wife, having children who believe.   Titus 1:6

From all of these we can see that children need kindness, gentleness, nurturing, encouragement, discipline, and instruction in the Lord. We'll start digging into what those words mean next.

What Do You Want for Your Children?

I want my children ___ (fill in the blank) ___.
- ___ To have a better life than I did growing up
- ___ To be successful
- ___ To be happy
- ___ To love and serve the Lord
- ___ Other

In talking with and listening to parents over the years, these are some things I've heard over and over again. No one will argue that these aren't good things. I too, have wanted good things for my children, and used to try to plan for them to have these things. However, at some point I began to contemplate this verse,

> For this cause a man shall leave his father and his mother and shall cleave to his wife, and they shall become one flesh.
> Genesis 2:24

Usually this verse is used in reference to marriage, but there is something in it for parents as well: "shall leave his father and his mother". Through this verse I realized that someday my children were going to grow up, leave home, and go on to live their own lives.

Understanding that began to change my understanding of my responsibility toward them, because it shifted my focus from them as children, and caused me to begin to look at them as future adults. It shifted my parenting goal from my children's happiness and personal fulfillment, to their future lives as mature, responsible adults. My responsibility was not to ensure their happiness, but to prepare them for the life they would live after they left home.

This might seem a small point, but it has been important to me. It's helped me to make some hard decisions, but more importantly, it's helped keep me from trying to impose my own plans onto their lives. It isn't my job to plan out their lives for them. That's the Lord's job. My job is to cooperate with the Lord in getting them to that point.

Children, Sin, and the D Word

When my daughter was a toddler, I happened to attend my husband's company Christmas dinner party. Across from me sat another company wife; also a Christian and a brand new mother. Having these two things in common, we had a lot to talk about. During the course of our conversation, she told me that her baby was so perfect that she could not believe that babies were born with sin. Babies were born sinless she felt, and learned sin as they grew up.

Nothing I said changed her mind. As I reflected on it later, I realized that she was setting herself up for a lot of heartache and disappointment. If babies are born sinless and learn sin as they grow up, then the responsibility for all sin falls onto their parents, for either teaching it themselves, or for allowing it to be taught to their children. What a horrible burden of guilt that would create!

This was one of those experiences that helped me to understand what sin really is. Sin is not doing bad things, rather, sin is the natural inclination toward Self and doing things our own way rather than God's way. It is true that babies are capable of learning a lot of bad behavior, but like all of us, babies are naturally self-centered rather than other-centered.

Selfishness is the manifestation of self-centeredness, and it is difficult to overcome, even for Christians who have been instructed to serve one another. I have often thought that my biggest obstacle to godliness was myself! The ability to not serve Self requires self-discipline. This does not come naturally; it must be learned.

I think that "discipline" is often misunderstood. Too often it is assumed to mean punishment, but do you remember the biblical definition from "To Love Their Children"?

Discipline. Strong's #3811, παιδευω, *paideuo* – to train up a child. i.e. educate, chasten (correct), nurture, instruct. Used thirteen times in the New Testament.

As Christian parents we need to train our children through instruction, correction, and nurturing. This pretty much flies in the face of the common modern parenting technique of permissiveness.

Understanding sin and biblical discipline helps us to understand these verses:

> *Discipline your son while there is still hope, and do not desire his death.* Prov. 18:18

> *Correct your son and he will give you comfort; he will also delight your soul.* Prov. 29:17

> *Train up a child in the way he should go, even when he is old he will not depart from it.* Prov. 22:6

> *Foolishness is bound up in the heart of a child; the rod of discipline will remove it far from him.* Prov. 22:15

Now, I'm not going to get caught up in the controversiality of "rod of discipline" and corporal punishment. What I am going to point out is that without discipline (instruction, correction, and nurturing), a child grows up into a selfish, impatient, self-indulgent adult. That is a very cruel thing to allow a child to become.

As parents we need to understand that children have a natural bend toward sin, and that we have a responsibility to influence them toward the other direction, toward the Lord. Through prayer, we need to discern their personal weaknesses and seek to turn these into strengths through instruction, modeling, and correction. All of this because we love them enough to do the tough things. Say no and mean it, don't renege on disciplinary measures such as "grounding" or "time out", and be consistent with the rules we make. But as hard as these things are to do, they are far better than the alternative.

Why I Homeschooled My Children

I can't write about loving our children and not mention homeschooling. In our study of Titus 2:3-5 we've gotten to Titus 2:4, "to love their children." We've seen that children need kindness, gentleness, nurturing, encouragement, discipline, and instruction in the Lord.

For me, the conviction to homeschool started with this verse:

> And you shall love the Lord your God with all your heart and with all your soul and with all your might. And these words which I am commanding you today, shall be on your heart; and you shall teach them diligently to your sons (children) and shall talk of them when you sit in your house and when you walk by the way and when you lie down and when you rise up.   Deut. 6:5-7

We started with faith and $75 for textbooks and supplies for our two children: a second grader and a sixth grader. I gave up teaching my Precept Upon Precept[1] Ladies Bible Study, which had been the absolute joy of my life, to be obedient to this conviction to homeschool. At that time I knew only one other person who homeschooled. Except for the support of my husband, who shared this conviction, I was pretty much on my own.

Understanding followed obedience. Although I gradually expanded my reasons for homeschooling, there were two which were especially important: worldview and socialization.

Worldview is the set of assumptions from which we view others and the world around us. These assumptions define:

~ Our beliefs about the existence and nature of God

~ Our understanding of the origin of the world (created or by chance?)
~ From where we believe knowledge comes (from God or man?)
~ How we view moral right and wrong (is there a standard or is it all relative?)
~ Our view of the origin and purpose of the human race (evolved or special creation?)
~ The meaning of human history (does God have a plan or do we create our own?)
~ What we believe happens after death (heaven or hell, reincarnation, nothingness?)

There are four basic worldviews which have different answers to these questions. Everyone has a form of one of them whether they recognize it or not, because everyone believes something. Consequently there is no worldview-neutral educational system; it is the nature of education to answer these questions. We teach and act on what we believe.

For example, from public education children will learn that the world and everything in it evolved, that humans have all the answers to life and can solve their own problems, that all religions are equal, to be silent about the Christian God, and to put Self first. I did not want my children taught these things as absolute truth.

The other reason I homeschooled was because of socialization. Every homeschool parent has been plagued with the question, "What about socialization?" Many respond with a long list of social activities in which their children are involved. My response was,

"Socialization *is* the reason I homeschool."

Why I Homeschooled My Children

I think most folks assume that "socialization" means "social interaction". To them homeschooling raises concerns about social isolation. However, the actual definition is -

Socialization — the process of learning the norms, values, behavior, beliefs, attitudes, and social skills of one's culture.

The question, then, becomes, "From whom do you want your children to learn a standard of behavior, beliefs, values, and attitudes?" If you are satisfied with the behavior and attitudes you see in children in the public schools, then that's the way for you to go. If you aren't, then public education is out of the question. The same question should also be applied to private schools being considered.

No one (besides the Lord) knows and loves your children better than you do, nor has their best interests at heart. I believe this is why parents are the best educators for their children. If a teaching degree was all that was necessary, then schools would be turning out well-adjusted geniuses. But they're not.

Homeschooling meant financial sacrifice for us because it meant living on only one income. It was a sacrifice of my own time and sometimes meant having to learn subject matter along with my children. However, one of my goals was for them to become independent learners, to know what information they needed, where to find it, and what to do with it once they got it. As their grade level progressed, they personally took on more of the responsibility, so that I didn't need mastery of every subject myself.

Now that both of my children have graduated from college and are out on their own, I can honestly say that I have no regrets. Nor can I think of a better way that I could have loved my children.

Encourage The Young Women

[1] Precept Upon Precept, Precept Ministries International, http://precept.org/

Public Education and Children as Missionaries

There is a curious protestation amongst Christians in regards to not sending our children to public schools. The argument's basic tenant is to view the public education system as a mission field, and that our presence is needed there as a witness. While I wholeheartedly agree that believing adults should serve as teachers, administrators, volunteers, and support staff in public education, the logic of applying this to our children escapes me.

Consider this: if you were having car trouble would you hand the tool box to your ten-year-old and expect him to fix it? Of course not! Why? Quite a few reasons: lack of knowledge, skills, experience, and ability to name a few.

Or this: if a young man or woman steps forward during the alter call on a Sunday morning and professes a call to missions, does the church simply hand them a suitcase and an airline ticket to Bogga-Bogga Land, wish them luck, and wave good bye? Of course not! Firstly there is prayer for discernment, and then the individual applies to seminary for training and a masters degree.

In the light of simple logic then, it absolutely escapes me why this seems a valid argument to keep children in public schools. I say this because I am often presented with it by other Christians when they learn I homeschooled. I usually make no reply, because I strongly believe that how one educates their children is a personal choice. Still, I puzzle over it because it never made any sense to me.

I finally concluded that it is just a quick comeback by those who don't want to consider homeschooling themselves, and for whom Christian schools aren't an option.

A few years ago, the whole argument took an even stranger turn when I happened to read an editorial on an Evangelical Christian website (which one, I can't remember for the life of me.) It was by a gentleman in Christian leadership whose wife was a teacher in a public school. The article pretty much took believers to task for suggesting that we abandon public education. In essence, he argued that if all Christian teachers and administrators left the public schools, then we would be abandoning an important mission field.

I confess that somehow I missed the part that equated the removal of our children from public schools, with Christian adults withdrawing from employment in public schools. As light and salt, we are to be witnesses in whatever dark corner of the world we find ourselves. However, in a system which is becoming increasingly hostile toward the God of the Bible, it takes spiritual maturity to be a witness.

This is why it is imperative that as Christian parents, we train our children in that spiritual maturity. To do this, we need to train up our children in an environment which nurtures Christian faith and beliefs, but always with an eye to their future witness as ambassadors for Christ.

Are Some Sins Worse Than Others?

This was a question that came to mind as I began researching the next concept in Titus 2:3-5 - purity.

> Encourage the young women to love their husbands, to love their children, to be sensible, <u>pure</u>, workers at home.
> Titus 2:4-5a

> Pure. Strong's #53, ’αγνος, *hagnos* - clean, i.e. (figuratively) innocent, modest, perfect. *The New Englishman's Greek Concordance and Lexicon*[1] states, "Holy, pure, undefiled, ceremonially and ethically." Used eight times in the New Testament. In the KJV translated as chaste, clear, pure.

When I first read the above definition in Strong's, the words "innocent" and "modest" made me think it meant sexual purity. Then I looked up all the verses in which it is used in the New Testament:

> In everything, you demonstrated yourselves to be <u>innocent</u> in the matter.   2 Cor. 7:11

> For I betrothed you to one husband, that to Christ I might present you as a <u>pure</u> virgin.   2 Cor. 11:2

> Finally brethren, whatever is true, whatever is honorable, whatever is right, whatever is <u>pure</u>... let your mind dwell on these things.   Phil 4:8

Do not lay hands upon anyone too hastily and thus share responsibility for the sins of others; keep yourself <u>free</u> from sin. 1 Tim. 5:22

But the wisdom from above is first <u>pure</u>. James 3:17

As they observe your <u>chaste</u> and respectful behavior.
1 Peter 3:2

And everyone who has this hope fixed on Him purifies himself, just as He is <u>pure</u>. 1 John 3:3

From these verses, I tried to glean as much information as I could, using my observation skills to question the text:

Who is pure in these verses?
 ~ The Corinthians in a particular matter
 ~ A virgin bride
 ~ Christ

What is pure?
 ~ Wisdom from above

Who is to be pure?
 ~ The Church
 ~ Timothy as a church leader
 ~ Believers in their thought lives
 ~ Believers in their behavior
 ~ Individual Believers

What is to be pure?
 ~ Our thoughts
 ~ Our behavior

Are Some Sins Worse Than Others?

How do we become/remain pure?
 ~ Guarding our thought life
 ~ Taking care upon whom we "lay hands"
 ~ Fixing our hope on Christ

Why are we to be pure?
 ~ To be like Jesus

Sexual purity is part of it, but 2 Cor. 7:11 says, "In everything," and Phil 4:8 says "Whatever." These broaden the definition to include a whole lot more. Which begs the question, is all sin equal?

James said:

> For whoever keeps the whole law and yet stumbles in one point, he has become guilty of all.   James 2:10

One might be quick to point out that as Christians, we aren't under the Law. Yet in context, James isn't speaking of the Mosaic law, but of Jesus' "new commandment":

> A new commandment I give to you, that you love one another, even as I have loved you, that you also love one another. By this all men will know that you are My disciples, if you have love for one another.
>
> John 13:34-35

The point I'm trying to make with the verse from James is that something isn't pure unless it's 100% pure. Even seemingly harmless sins taint our purity and our testimony, for example, telling "white lies," or not returning borrowed items. And it's not only our outward actions, but also our thought lives (see Matt. 5:28 in addition to Phil. 4:8), and the words we speak (see James 3:8-12) which are part of the purity equation.

Time for self-reflection:

~ Are some sins okay under certain circumstances?

~ Do some sins seem more or less acceptable than others?

~ Do I view all sin the same?

~ What "little" sins do I make excuses for so as to justify them?

Every sin can be repented of and forgiven by God except one. The one sin that keeps people out of heaven is rejecting Jesus Christ. If we are not guilty of this, then we can strive to be pure in all other things. As Paul said:

> *For we are the temple of the living God; just as God said, "I will dwell in them and walk among them; and I will be their God and they shall be My people. Therefore come out from their midst and be separate," says the Lord. "And do not touch what is unclean; and I will welcome you, and I will be a father to you, and you shall be sons and daughters to Me," says the Lord Almighty. Therefore, having these promises beloved, let us cleanse ourselves from all defilement of flesh and spirit, perfecting holiness in the fear of God.*
> 2 Cor. 6:16b – 7:1

Guardians of the Household

Housewife. Homemaker. Domestic Engineer. Stay-At-Home-Mom. SAHM. The term has evolved somewhat over the years, but the concept is the same. It refers to women whose occupation is to oversee and manage the domestic business of the family.

For reasons I won't address here, the concept of women as keepers of the home has fallen out of favor in modern times. Women's traditional roles and responsibilities have lost their value and esteem, as if what men do is more important than what women have traditionally done. As a sad consequence of buying into this fallacy, women have stepped down from a position of power in the name of equality.

In spite of rumors and accusations, the Bible never portrays women as unequal. The deeper we dig into Scripture, the more clear this will become; but for now, let's take a closer look at the next term in the verses we've been studying in Titus.

> *To be sensible, pure, <u>workers at home</u>, kind, subject to their own husbands, that the word of God may not be dishonored.*
> *Titus 2:5*

> Workers at home, rendered "keepers at home" in the KJV. Strong's #3626, οικουρος, *oikouros* [from #3624, *oikos* - dwelling, family, home, and *ouros* - a guard] - stayer at home, domestically inclined, keeper at home. A footnote to this term in *Vincent's Word Studies of the New Testament* states, "The meaning is not stayers at home, but keepers or guardians of the household."[1]

Although *oikouros* is used only one time in the New Testament, a cross reference will be helpful in further understanding it.

> *Therefore I want younger widows to get married, bear children, <u>keep house</u>, and give the enemy no occasion for reproach.* 1 Timothy 5:14

> Keep House. Strong's #3616, οικοδεσποτεω, *oikodespoteo* – to be head of (i.e. rule) a family, guide the house. From Zodhiates[2], "To govern or manage a household or the domestic affairs of a family."

It is interesting to note that our English word "despot" comes from the Greek *despoteo* in the above term. Although "despot" has somewhat negative connotations, what we see in these verses is that God has given wives the absolute authority and the full responsibility for the business of managing home and family.

Biblical models? Think of the Proverbs 31 Woman: wife, mother, mistress, manager, administrator, overseer, organizer, purchaser, weaver, chef, baker, gardener, garment maker, philanthropist, diplomat, counselor, teacher, helpmate; who did it all so well that she even managed to have a successful home business. How did this effect her husband? He was known at the gates and sat among the elders of the land (verse 23).

Of course, the Proverbs 31 Woman had a large household with servants to manage. Yet even in our smaller homes we have the responsibility to create a welcoming, peaceful, restful atmosphere for our husbands and guests, and a loving, caring, nurturing environment for our children. And not only are we to create it, but we are to maintain and guard it as well.

Guardians of the Household

Our role as guardians becomes especially significant when we consider our children. My Sisters in Christ, do you not understand the power we have as Keepers at Home to mold the hearts and minds of the next generation?

> *Train up a child in the way he should go, even when he is old he will not depart from it.*   Prov. 22:6

One thing must be noted however. It is that authority never comes without accountability. If we understand that the Bible never contradicts itself, then we must understand that neither does a wife stand alone and independent in her authority over the home and family. Our God is a God of order, and there is an order in the family structure which includes both husband and wife. However, we will look more closely at that structure when we look at being "subject to their own husbands."

---

[1] Marvin R. Vincent, D.D, *Word Studies of the New Testament* (Eerdman's Publishing, Grand Rapids, MI, reprinted 1989) 842

[2] Spiros Zodhiates, *The Complete Word Study Dictionary: New Testament* (AMG Publishers, Chattanooga, 1992) 1030

Influencing Others

As leaders of the home, women have a profound influence on the other members of it. This can be for good or not. The Bible addresses this influence in the next word of the verse we're studying:

> To be sensible, pure, workers at home, <u>kind</u>, subject to their own husbands, that the word of God may not be dishonored.
> Titus 2:5

> Kind. Strong's #18, αγαθος, agathos — "good" (in any sense, often as noun), benefit, good, well. *The Complete Word Study Dictionary* adds, "Good, in respect to operation or influence on others, i.e., useful, beneficial, profitable. Of persons, benevolent, beneficent."[1]

Agathos is found 102 times in the New Testament and is usually translated as "good." It can refer to God, people, or things. Of these, I've tried to pick out cross references that will be useful to us in the context of Titus 2:5, i.e. being kind.

Our good kindness manifests itself in three interrelated ways.

1. Our actions:

> For we are His workmanship, created in Christ Jesus for <u>good works</u>, which God prepared beforehand, that we should walk in them.
> Eph. 2:10

> So that you may walk in a manner worthy of the Lord, to please Him in all respects, bearing fruit in every <u>good work</u> and increasing in the knowledge of God.
> Col. 1:10

> But rather by means of <u>good works</u>, as befits women making a claim to godliness.   1 Tim 2:10

2. Our words:

> Now may our Lord Jesus Christ Himself and God our Father ... comfort and strengthen your hearts in every good work and <u>word</u>.   2 Thes. 2:16a-17

> Let no unwholesome word proceed from your mouth, but only such a <u>word as is good</u> for edification according to the need of the moment, that it may give grace to those who hear.
>   Eph. 4:29

3. Our conscience:

> The good man out of the <u>good treasure of his heart</u> brings forth what is <u>good</u>; and the evil man out of the evil treasure brings forth what is evil; for his mouth speaks from that which fills his heart.   Luke 6:45

> And keep a <u>good conscience</u> so that in the thing in which you are slandered, those who revile your good behavio<u>r</u> in Christ may be put to shame.   1 Peter 3:16

Why our conscience? Because if we are harboring anger, bitterness, guilt, wrong motives, etc., it will affect our attitude, which in turn affects our words and actions. As guardians of the home, it is imperative that we guard our own hearts and minds; primarily because we are to influence others toward godliness, but also because it sets an example for our children to follow.

What prevents us from being kind and having a good influence on others? We could make a pretty practical list from the following verses in 2 Timothy 2:

Influencing Others

> (Don't) wrangle about words, which is useless and leads to the ruin of the hearers. 2 Tim. 2:14

> Avoid worldly and empty chatter, for it will lead to further ungodliness, and their talk will spread like gangrene.
> 2 Tim. 2:16–17

> Refuse foolish and ignorant speculations, knowing that these produce quarrels, and the Lord's bondservant must not be quarrelsome. 2 Tim. 2:23–24

One thing I noticed in our homeschool group was that some women would engage in these things when they thought their children weren't listening. I learned to never underestimate what kids pick up! It always came out later in their children's attitudes, if not words and behavior.

I learned to take this verse to heart:

> Guard, through the Holy Spirit who dwells in us, the treasure which has been entrusted to you. 2 Tim. 1:14

As wives and mothers we have been entrusted with a great treasure: our families and our homes. May we never forget that we have a godly mandate to guard them not only with our actions, but with our words and attitudes as well.

---

[1] Spiros Zodhiates, *The Complete Word Study Dictionary: New Testament* (AMG Publishers, Chattanooga, 1992) 62

Feminism's 4-Letter Word

Actually, this is a subject that no one likes - submission. It is associated with subservience, subjugation, inferiority, inequality; things that make most of us bristle. Yet, as you've been reading through these lessons on Titus 2, you should see a pattern: our modern concepts of many words used in the Bible are a far cry from their original, biblical meaning.

To understand what the Bible is really saying, we need to give it a fair hearing. We need to lay down our prejudices and preconceived ideas, and give Scripture a chance to speak for itself. Anyone who has ever been misunderstood wishes for this very thing. Indeed, this is what a court of law is supposed to do before pronouncing a verdict. This is what we need to do in order to understand what God is trying to tell us through His Word.

Consider this next phrase in Titus 2:5:

> To be sensible, pure, workers at home, kind, <u>subject to their own husbands</u>, that the word of God may not be dishonored.
> Titus 2:5

There are three Greek words to research here: subject, their own, and husbands. This chapter will begin to look at the first one.

> Subject. Strong's #5293, ὑποτασω, *hupotasso* - [from 5259, ὑπο, *hupo* - under, and 5021, τασω, *tasso* - to place, set, appoint, arrange, order]. "To place under in an orderly fashion"[1] Used 40 times in the New Testament.

In the ancient world, *hupotasso* was used in two contexts. First, as a military term. It referred to the ordering of troops under the command of a military leader. This is an important point in understanding submission, because anyone who has ever been in the military knows that just because someone is an officer doesn't mean they are smarter, braver, better, or in any way superior as human beings. The position serves as a strictly structural function to keep order. Without order, nothing could be accomplished and the group would deteriorate in chaos.

Hupotasso also had a non-military use in Koine Greek, referring to a voluntary acceptance of a subordinate position. It implied cooperation, assumption of responsibility, and the carrying of a burden.

Applying this to our verse in Titus 2, we see that submission has nothing to do with status, but everything to do with function. Its meaning implies cooperation, and cooperation implies common goals. Two important goals of a Christian marriage should be to honor and serve the Lord as a couple, and to raise children to know and serve the Lord. If husband and wife are working independently toward different goals friction and struggle result.

If we lived in a perfect world, submission wouldn't be an issue because we would all operate according to God's perfect plan for humanity. Indeed, submission was not given to wives until after the Fall.

> *And he shall rule over you.*   Gen. 3:16

However, we live in a sinful world, where everyone wants their own way. It is our fallen nature to think we're usually right. That's why no one likes the idea of submission. Achieving order (in any venue: military, athletic, classroom, family, etc.) requires enough self-discipline to set aside personal desires and opinions for the sake of something greater. If either party's focus is only on serving Self and meeting Self's needs, then conflict occurs.

Feminism's 4-Letter Word

Something else we need to understand, is that the husband is not free to rule over his wife in any way he pleases. His position is not given to him to lord it over his wife, nor to feel superior, nor to use her to try to achieve his own personal ambitions. Submission also applies to him. How? We'll look at that next.

---

[1] Spiros Zodhiates, *The Complete Word Study Dictionary: New Testament* (AMG Publishers, Chattanooga, 1992) 1427

Submission For Husbands? You've Got to be Kidding

When it comes to discussing biblical submission in marriage, the idea of mutual submission often comes up. This is based upon this verse:

> And be subject to one another in the fear of Christ.
> Eph 5:21

Unfortunately, applying it to husbands and wives is taking it out of context. It is actually part of a set of instructions for Church members. Instructions for husbands and wives begin with a new paragraph in the next verse.

The problem with trying to apply mutual submission to marriage is that it doesn't resolve certain practical problems such as a stalemate. Even in the secular world, some appointed person (e.g. committee chair or judge) serves as a tie-breaker. Scripture makes no allowances for such a tie-breaker in marriage.

I think a stronger argument for submission of husbands can be made here:

> But I want you to understand that Christ is the head of every man, and the man is the head of a woman, and God is the head of Christ.
> 1 Cor.11:3

Notice the chain of command. A husband is expected to be submissive to his own head, Jesus Christ, who is subject to God the Father. God has given the man very specific instructions for his role as husband.

> Husbands, love your wives just as Christ also loved the church and gave Himself up for her; that He might sanctify

> *her, having cleansed her by the washing of the water with the word, that He might present to Himself the church in all her glory, having no spot or wrinkle or any such thing; but that she should be holy and blameless.* Eph. 5:25-27

Note the "as," which indicates a comparison. Christ's goals for the church are to be the husband's goals for his wife. He is to love her to the point of sacrificing himself for her spiritual growth and purity, keeping in mind that when she is presented to the Lord, she will be a reflection of him. As the wife is to guard the spiritual purity of her household, so the husband is to guard the spiritual purity of his wife.

> *So husbands ought also to love their own wives as their own bodies. He who loves his wife loves himself; for no one ever hated his own flesh, but nourishes and cherishes it just as Christ also does the church, because we are members of His body. "For this cause a man shall leave his father and mother, and shall cleave to his wife, and the two shall become one flesh."* Eph. 5:28-31

Let's face it, human nature wants to be comfortable. We all want to be warm and well fed. No one likes pain or inconvenience. The Bible says that as spiritual head, the husband is responsible for his wife's comfort and well-being. He is to treat her as he would himself, because they are in fact one flesh. Not only that, according to verse 25 he is to deny himself, if necessary, to achieve this. In other words, he is to put his wife first.

> *You husbands likewise, live with your wives in an understanding way, as with a weaker vessel, since she is a woman, and grant her honor as a fellow heir of the grace of life, so that your prayers my not be hindered.* 1 Peter 3:7

To be understanding, a husband must have knowledge of his wife's feelings, concerns, needs, etc. and order their lives accordingly.

First, let's look at the term "weaker". I realize this word is much debated, even argued, amongst Christians. What I would like to point out here, is that the term is comparative. The verse does not say men are strong and women are weak. Men are weak too, which is why they need to submit to their own spiritual head. However, because husbands are required to lay down their lives for the spiritual well-being of their wives, they must have greater self-control and self-discipline.

The word "vessel" refers to a cup or dish. I like to think of it as fine china. Fine china is not made for rough handling; it is treated with care. Husbands are to treat their wives with gentleness and care. Also, he is to grant her honor.

> Honor. Strong's #5092, τιμη, *time* - value, esteem, reverence

Husbands are to value and respect their wives. Why? Because their wives are fellow heirs with an equal share in the inheritance of the Kingdom (Gal. 3:28). In addition, note that there are spiritual consequences for a husband's disobedience; his prayers will be hindered.

Christian wives, wouldn't you be willing to submit to a husband who respected and treated you as the Lord commanded him to? Or do you still have doubts about that word "submit"? We'll take a closer look at it in the next chapter.

Submission: Biblical Inequality?

I've come to realize that part of the problem women have with submission is because the word carries connotations of inequality. Leadership means telling others what to do; the superior gives the orders and the subordinate obeys, right? Giving in to someone else is as a sign of inferiority.

While these are commonly accepted concepts in the modern world, they are examples of what I call "worldly" thinking rather than "Wordly thinking."

Hopefully, you have seen a pattern as you've been reading. The biblical definitions of many words are not the same as the worldly definitions, for example: temperance, love, and encouragement.

As Christians, one thing we must guard against when trying to interpret the Bible, is assuming that the world's definitions are the only correct definitions. If we do, then we are going to reach wrong conclusions. "Submission" is a case in point. And sadly, not only do women often buy into the idea that the biblical submission means an inequality between the sexes, many men do too.

We've already taken a look at the biblical definition of submit (subject) in "Feminism's 4-Letter Word". We saw that it does not refer to a hierarchy of importance; rather, it refers to orderliness. However, I'd like to give you a few more verses to contemplate, along with some observations about them.

> And God created man in His own image, in the image of God He created them; male and female He created them.
> Gen. 1:27

"Man" here is Strong's #120, 'adam, which refers to the species of mankind. God created human beings as male and female in His own image.

> *For this cause a man shall leave his father and mother and shall cleave to his wife, and they shall become one flesh.*
>
> Gen. 2:24

"Man" here is a different Hebrew word, Strong's #376, *ysh*, meaning a male person. Man as an individual was not created complete in himself. He is incomplete without woman. Only together are they whole.

> *There is neither Jew nor Greek, there is neither slave nor freeman, there is neither male nor female; for you are all one in Christ Jesus.*   Gal. 3:28

God sees us not in ranks, but as one. The Bible only distinguishes between two classes of people: those who believe and accept the truth, and those who reject it.

> *You husbands ... grant her honor as a fellow heir of the grace of life, so that your prayers may not be hindered.*
>
> 1 Peter 3:7

Husbands are warned against treating their wives as inferior. She is a fellow heir (Strong's #4789, *sugkleronomos* - joint heir, participant in common.)

The bottom line in Bible study is to let the Bible define the terms, not let the terms define the Bible. To assume that the Bible teaches that women are inferior to men is an incorrect interpretation. An incorrect interpretation does not make the Bible wrong; it only makes the interpreter wrong.

Conclusion? If God sees men and women as equal, then "submission" does not indicate inequality, but refers to something else. Next, we need to discover what that something else is.

Changing Our Husbands

I was in a ladies Sunday school class several years ago where the topic of discussion was husbands who didn't go to church. Several women complained that because their husbands refused to go to church, the entire burden of spiritual leadership for their family fell upon themselves. One woman, however, had a different approach. She shared this with us:

> She said, "One Sunday morning I got up at the usual time, but instead of getting myself and the children ready for church, I sat at the kitchen table in my bathrobe, drinking my coffee and reading the Sunday paper.
>
> After awhile, my husband asked, 'Isn't it time for you to get ready to go to church?'
>
> 'Well, dear' I replied sweetly, 'You are the spiritual head of this family. From now on the children and I are going to follow your lead.' "
>
> She told us that from that Sunday on, her husband had never missed a service.

After reading "Submission for Husbands? You've Got to be Kidding", most of us can probably point out all the times in which our husbands fail at these things. On the other hand, we have to admit that neither are we perfectly submissive and supportive of them. I know I'm not.

So what do we do when our husbands are not acting in a godly manner, or aren't following biblical principles when they make decisions affecting their wives and families? What then? Most of us have probably tried arguing, but how effective is that?

Here is a verse to consider:

> *In the same way, you wives, be submissive to your own husbands so that even if any of them are disobedient to the word, they may be won without a word by the behavior of their wives, as they observe your chaste and respectful behavior.*
> 1 Peter 3:1-2

Who is being addressed? Wives

What about? Husbands who are disobedient to the word. I've heard some say this refers to unsaved husbands, but the principle applies to saved husbands as well.

What is she to do? Behave in a chaste and respectful manner toward him.

> Chaste. Strong's #53, ἁγνος, *hagnos* - properly clean, that is, (figuratively) innocent, modest, perfect, pure. From the same root as the word translated "holy."
>
> Respectful. Strong's #5401, φοβος, *phobos* - This word has two definitions, depending on context. 1) fear, dread, or terror. 2) Respect for one's husband.
>
> Manner. Strong's #391, αναστροφη, *anastrophe* - manner of life, conduct, behavior, deportment. Translated as "conversation" in the KJV.

How is she to do this? (This is the hard part.) Without a word.

Why? Note the "in the same way" at the beginning of verse 1, above. We should immediately ask, in the same way as what? The previous verses answer that queston.

> *For you have been called for this purpose, since Christ also suffered for you, leaving an example for you to follow in His steps, "Who committed no sin, nor was any deceit found in His mouth"; and while being reviled, He did not revile in return; while suffering, He uttered no threats, but kept entrusting Himself to Him who judges righteously.*
>
> 1 Peter 2:21-23

Jesus, who suffered horrendously, left an example for when we, too, are treated harshly or unfairly (verses 19 and 20). Or, "in the same way", for suffering when our husbands are disobedient to the Word. Rather than speaking out, Jesus trusted the Father. Wives too, are to trust the Lord rather than try to correct their husbands with words.

It is the Holy Spirit who convicts and corrects. Too often, we get in the way by trying to influence a situation ourselves. God's will for all is salvation first, followed by growing in Christlikeness. He is working all things toward this end. (Rom. 8:28-29). In our marriages, we can cooperate with Him by quietly and lovingly supporting our husbands, confident in the knowledge that no matter how difficult the situation seems, nothing is impossible for God (Luke 18:27). Our spiritual leadership is to be by example, not words.

It all boils down to trust. During times we feel we cannot trust our husbands, can we trust the Lord to work in that situation? Here are some verses I hold onto for my husband whenever I suffer in this manner:

> *For I am confident of this very thing, that He who began a good work in you will perfect it until the day of Christ Jesus.* Philippians 1:6

Encourage The Young Women

For it is God who is at work in you, both to will and to work for His good pleasure. Do all things without grumbling or disputing, that you may prove yourselves to be blameless and innocent, children of God ... holding fast to the word of life.
Philippians 2:13-16

Submission: Where Do We Draw the Line?

Everyone struggles with submission, and yet no one is free from it. In the Bible we see Jesus submitting to the Father, the church submitting to Christ, men submitting to Christ, women submitting to their husbands, children submitting to their parents. Even in the secular world submission exists, whether to employers, teachers, civil authorities, traffic laws, etc. When we voluntarily agree to abide by the various authority structures in our lives, we are (theoretically at least) protected from chaos and its consequences. If we rebel, the integrity of the structure is at risk.

This, of course, assumes that the structure is set in place for the good of those who must function within it. The problem is that we live in a fallen world. Because of that, we often find abuses of any given authority structure, from those who use their power to promote themselves at the expense of the ones under them, to those who rebel and refuse to abide by the "rules" for the sake of individuality.

How does this apply to marriage? Because we are looking at a God-ordained structure occupied by imperfect humans. Under the best of circumstances, both parties try their best to cooperate. Commonly, one, the other, or both, refuse to cooperate and insist on their own way. Occasionally, one abuses both the structure as well as their spouse. Consider this verse:

> But as the church is subject to Christ, so also the wives ought to be to their husbands in everything.   Eph. 5:24

> Everything. Strong's #3956, πας, *pas* - all, any, every, the whole, thoroughly

Everything? As in every thing? A selfish, thoughtless husband is bad enough, but what about the husband who is physically abusive? Is a wife supposed to submit to that? Or to pornography? Or to drugs?

Tragically, some would say "yes." However, I absolutely do not believe that this verse teaches blind submission on the part of wives. For example, if something is illegal, then she is not to submit. What am I basing this on? Common sense surely, but also on the Scripture itself.

> *Let every person be in subjection to the governing authorities. For there is no authority except from God, and those which exist are established by God.*   Romans 13:1

If we submit to illegal activity in our home, then according to this verse, we are being disobedient to God as well as the law. For some crimes, such as domestic violence, we may be the victims. For other crimes, such as illegal drugs, child abuse, or pornography, we become accomplices at the risk of going to prison and losing our children. According to this verse, we are accountable not only to the law, but to the Lord for what takes place in our home.

This points to what we've already seen in studying Titus chapter 2, that a wife's God-appointed role is to be the guardian of her home. She is not simply guarding her home for her own well-being, but especially for her children's. Not only is she to protect them from harm, but because whatever goes on in the home will become their concept of "normal." They will grow up and live out what they have seen modeled by their parents.

Blind submission? No. Biblical submission? Yes. And always with an eye to the Lord, trusting that He is accomplishing a greater good because of it. (Rom. 8:28-29).

Submission To Whom?

> *To be sensible, pure, workers at home, kind, subject <u>to their own husbands</u>, that the word of God may not be dishonored.*
> Titus 2:5

> To their own. Strong's #2398, ιδιος, *idios* - pertaining to self, i.e. one's own

Sadly, I've seen that little phrase overlooked when it comes to interpreting this verse. Why is it important? Because of what this phrase doesn't say. It does not say that women are to be subject to men, it says that wives are to be subject to their own husbands.

True, the Greek word for "husbands" here is "man."

> Husband. Strong's #435, 'ανηρ, *aner* - a man. Translated as man, husband, fellow, sir.

In the context of this verse, however, it refers to a woman's husband ("their *own* man"). This is reinforced by cross references:

> *Wives be subject <u>to your own</u> husbands as to the Lord.*
> Eph. 5:22

> *In the same way, you wives, be submissive <u>to your own</u> husbands.*
> 1 Peter 3:1a

What this points to is the uniqueness of the marital relationship, not an inequality of the sexes. The distinction within the church is not between men and women, but between husbands and wives.

Christians are to show respect to one another no matter their place or position. Yet within the church, the relationship of husband and wife is unique and privileged. It is to be an illustration to the world of the relationship of Christ and the Church (Eph. 5:22-33).

The question for each one of us is, when people look at my marriage, what do they see? Does it give them an accurate picture of Christ and the Church? Probably not, especially if our husbands are unsaved, backslidden, or spiritually immature. What do we do then? Unfortunately, no one can change another person. No amount of reasoning, nagging, coaxing, threatening, or putting down of one's foot will change them. In fact, when we use these techniques, what does the world see? They see one partner trying to coerce and dominate the other. There is no equality in that.

The Bible never teaches dominance in the husband/wife relationship; rather, it teaches the laying down of one's life. Indeed, Jesus said this proves that we belong to Him (John 13:34-35). Husbands are to lay down their lives for their wives (Eph 5:25), and wives are to lay down their lives for their husbands (Eph. 5:22). Neither is conditional on the other.

Easy? No. When I'm struggling with this, the following verses help. I hope they will be of help to you too.

> *Do nothing from selfishness or empty conceit, but with humility of mind let each of you regard one another as more important than himself; do not merely look out for your own personal interests, but also for the interests of others. Have this attitude in yourselves which was also in Christ Jesus, who although He existed in the form of God, did not regard equality with God a thing to be grasped, but emptied Himself, taking the form of a bond-servant.*
>
> *Philippians 2:3-7a*

Dishonoring The Word of God

Structuring is a Bible study technique which visually organizes a passage. It is similar to outlining, but instead of numbering the main points and subpoints, phrases are arranged in columns, with each column referring back to the phrase being described or modified. Its purpose is to analyze the thought structure. It is helpful because it develops a visual record of the author's flow of thought, regardless of grammatical structure (which isn't the same in all languages.)

As an example, let's take a passage which ought to be pretty familiar by now.

> Older men are to be temperate, dignified, sensible, sound in faith, in love, in perseverance. Older women likewise, are to be reverent in their behavior, not malicious gossips, nor enslaved to much wine, teaching what is good that they may encourage the young women to love their husbands, to love their children, to be sensible, pure, workers at home, kind, being subject to their own husbands, that the word of God may not be dishonored. Titus 2:2-5

I begin observing the text by asking it questions: who, what, where, when, why, and how. Structuring helps me find the answers, because it forces me to determine how the phrases and thoughts relate to one another. As I write out the text, I organize it so that I can see the flow of thought. As I see how each phrase stems from another phrase, the context becomes clearer.

On the next page I have structured Titus 2:2-5 for you. I like to write out my who, what, where, when, why, and how questions as I analyze each verse.

Encourage The Young Women

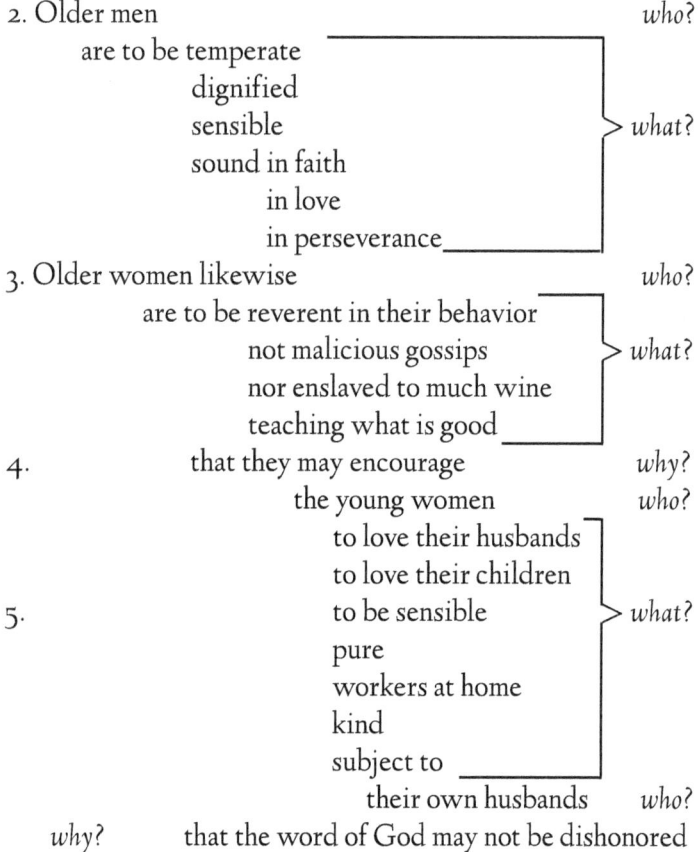

As you can see, this nicely organizes the various points into handy lists.

Who is being addressed? Older men
What are they to do? Be temperate, dignified, sensible, etc.
Who else? Older women
How? likewise (the same way)
What are they to do? Be reverent, etc.
Why? that the word of God may not be dishonored

Dishonoring The Word of God

Sometimes it is a challenge to decide exactly what a phrase is referring back to, such as the phrase "that the word of God may not be dishonored." It answers why something needs to be done. But what? Wives being subject to their husbands? Does it refer to the entire list of what young women are to do? Or, does it refer to "teaching what is good"? Does it mean all of the above?

I can't decide. Perhaps there is some clue in the meaning of the word.

> Dishonored. Strong's #987, βλασφημεω, blasphemeo - to vilify, to speak impiously, blaspheme, defame, revile, speak evil of, speak against, malign.

What in Titus 2:2-5 would cause people to criticize the Word of God? My next step is to see how *blasphemeo* is used elsewhere in the New Testament.

> *You who boast in the Law, through your breaking the Law, do you dishonor God? For "The name of God is <u>blasphemed</u> among the Gentiles because of you," just as it is written.*
> Romans 2:23-24

> *Let all who are under the yoke of slavery regard their own masters as worthy of all honor so that the name of God and our doctrine may not <u>be spoken against</u>.*   1 Cor. 6:1

> *And in all this, they are surprised that you do not run with them into the same excess of dissipation, and they <u>malign</u> you.*   1 Peter 4:4

> *And many will follow their sensuality, and because of them the way of truth will be <u>maligned</u>.*   2 Peter 2:2

One common thread I see in these cross references is that it is our actions which either honor God or dishonor Him. Returning to our passage in Titus 2:3-5, we see a list of behaviors which honor the word of God. To see how we might dishonor it, let us consider the opposites:

Older women dishonor the word of God by:
- ∼ constant silliness
- ∼ dishonesty
- ∼ impulsiveness
- ∼ self-indulgence
- ∼ irreverence
- ∼ pessimism
- ∼ unkindness
- ∼ criticizing others
- ∼ encouraging others to do the same by their words and their example

Younger women dishonor the word of God by:
- ∼ disrespecting their husbands
- ∼ putting themselves before their children
- ∼ silliness
- ∼ immodesty
- ∼ neglect of home
- ∼ unkindness
- ∼ argumentative with husbands
- ∼ rebelliousness

All these things describe the opposites of the behaviors listed in Titus 2:3-5.

Often we choose a behavior or an attitude to get our point across to another person. Perhaps what we aren't always aware of, is that we are also making a point about our God.

Dishonoring The Word of God

I admit that I don't keep this in mind often enough. Situations and circumstances come and go and are often forgotten, but how we deal with these leaves behind an impression not only about us, but also about the word of God. This is something to keep in mind as we ponder our course of action in working things out. We are going to make an impression one way or another. The question we need to continually ask ourselves is, what kind?

"That She Respect Her Husband"

Before we wrap up our study of Titus 2:3-5, there is one more verse at which I would like to take a look. It's in Ephesians, but it is very much related to what we are studying.

> *And let the wife see to it that she <u>respect</u> her husband.*
> *Eph. 5:33*

We first looked at this word in "Changing Our Husbands." Do you remember this verse?

> *In the same way, you wives, be submissive to your own husbands so that even if any of them are disobedient to the word, they may be won without a word by the behavior of their wives, as they observe your chaste and <u>respectful</u> behavior.*
> *1 Peter 3:1-2*

> Respectful. Strong's #5401, φοβος, *phobos* - This word has two definitions, depending on context. 1) fear, dread, or terror. 2) Respect for one's husband.

Noah Webster's 1828 Dictionary puts it like this,

To view or consider with some degree of reverence; to esteem as possessed of real worth.[1]

The question then is, "Do you see your husband as having real worth?" Surely we can readily agree, but if we are in a difficult marriage, perhaps not. At the very least he possesses value because he was created in God's image. If for no other reason than that he deserves respect.

Encourage The Young Women

Often when women get together to fellowship the conversation will include marriages and husbands. This isn't surprising, but I become uncomfortable when husbands' mistakes become sources of amusing anecdotes. Even worse is if these sessions turn into a camaraderie of fault finding.

"But it was only a joke," someone might protest, or "I just needed to get that off my chest." I admit those ideas tempt me too, but here is one of the verses that always stops me:

> *Treat others the same way you want them to treat you.*
> Luke 6:31

How do I feel when my faults and mistakes are being discussed behind my back or being used as the butt of a joke? Let's take it a step further:

> *Above all, keep fervent in your love for one another, because love <u>covers</u> a multitude of sins.* 1 Peter 4:8

> Covers. Strong's #2572, καλυπτω, *kalupto* - to envelop, wrap around as bark, cover over, hide. To hinder the knowledge of a thing.

In other words, Christian love does not expose the faults of others: not for a joke, not in order to feel better by venting our frustrations.

The reward for respecting our husbands is a very precious one - trust.

> *The heart of her husband trusts in her, and he will find no lack of gain. She does him good and not evil all the days of her life.* Proverbs 31: 11-12

"That She Respect Her Husband"

Time for reflection:

∼ Do my words, attitudes, and actions do my husband good or evil?

∼ Does he trust me with his hopes and dreams? With his feelings and fears?

∼ Does he feel more comfortable spending an evening at home, or out with the boys?

To answer why this is even important, I think it might be helpful to examine the intent and design of marriage. Coming up, we'll take a look at the very first marriage and what the Lord had to say about it.

---

[1]Noah Webster, *American Dictionary of the English Language*, 1928 edition (Foundation for American Christian Education, San Francisco, 1995)

The Spiritually Mature Woman
A Summary of Titus 2:3-5

Before we finish up this section, I'd like to take time to summarize what we've learned. We've spent quite a lot of time focusing on details, so it's finally time to step back and see how it all fits together.

> Older women likewise are to be reverent in their behavior, not malicious gossips, nor enslaved to much wine, teaching what is good, that they may encourage the young women to love their husbands, to love their children, to be sensible, pure, workers at home, kind, being subject to their own husbands that the word of God may not be dishonored. Titus 2:3-5

"Likewise" in verse 3 points back to the previous verse.

> Older men are to be temperate, dignified, sensible, sound in faith, in love, in perseverance. Titus 2:2

In context, Paul is writing to Titus. Why?

> For this reason I left you in Crete, that you might set in order what remains and appoint elders in every city as I directed you. Titus 1:5

The rest of the letter tells how those things are to be done, so that in the end, we have a mental picture of what a spiritually mature, orderly church looks like. How do women fit in?

<u>As Leaders and Teachers:</u>

~ Temperate – exercise self-control over emotions and desires

- Dignified – having self-respect in conduct

- Sensible – self-controlled in opinions and passions

- Sound in faith – acts on an accurate conviction of God's truth

- Sound in love – seeks the welfare of those around her

- Sound in perseverance – endures difficulties with hope

- Reverent in her behavior - manner of life reflects her total dedication to God

- Not a malicious gossip – doesn't speak ill of others

- Nor enslaved to much wine – free from physical, mental, or emotional addiction

- Teaching what is good – teaches how to be good, not just to do good

- Encouraging – others toward a changed, more godly life

<u>As Wives and Mothers:</u>

- Love their husbands – have genuine affection toward

- Love their children - have a gentle, tender, caring maternal bond

- Sensible – self-controlled in opinions and passions

- Pure – free from sin in action, thoughts, and attitude

A Summary of The Spiritually Mature Woman

- ∼ Workers at home – to be managers and guardians of their households

- ∼ Kind – having a good influence by actions, words, and conscience

- ∼ Subject to own husband – to willingly order her household for her husband

- ∼ Respect her husband – (Eph. 5:33) regards him as worthy of her esteem

<u>The Result?</u>

- ∼ God is glorified and His Word is honored.

And that is what the Church is supposed to be about.

Genesis
Chapters 1-3

Genesis 1: An Overview of Creation

The next thing I'd like to do is to take a look at the very first marriage. This is found in the first two chapters of Genesis, but to interpret these chapters correctly, we need to understand something about the style of ancient Hebrew writing. I say this because at a cursory reading, these first two chapters of Genesis appear to be contradictory.

One of the premises of inductive Bible study is that the Bible never contradicts itself. If it appears to, then we need to dig deeper. For Genesis One and Two it is helpful to understand that the first chapter is an overview, or summary of creation. Chapter Two then goes back to cover the specifics relevant to us. It fills in the details.

This same style is seen in the book of Daniel, where Nebuchadnezzar's statue dream in chapter two gives an overview of the future. Subsequent dreams and visions begin to fill in the details. This literary technique is also used in the book of Revelation. Many read that book in a chronological fashion, but it makes more sense to read it as more than one account of the end, each account focusing on different details.

In Genesis 1, we are given an overview of the creation of the human race.

> Then God said,"Let Us make man in Our image, according to Our likeness; and let them rule ... over all the earth ... And God created man in His own image, in the image of God He created him; male and female He created them. And God blessed them; and God said to them, "Be fruitful and multiply, and fill the earth, and subdue it; and rule over ... every living thing that moves on the earth. Then God said, "Behold, I have given you every plant yielding seed that is on the surface of all the earth, and every tree which has fruit

yielding seed; it shall be food for you ... And God saw all that He had made, and behold it was very good.
Gen. 1: 26-29, 31

I've condensed these verses a little for the sake of space, but let's look at the word "man."

> Man. Strong's #120, אדם, *adam* - man, mankind, human, Adam as the first man.

How do we know that "man" refers to the human race here and not the gender? First, because the plural pronoun "them" is used. Secondly, because of *how* God created them - male and female.

What did He create them to do (verse 28)?

∼ Create families
∼ Populate the earth
∼ Subdue and rule over the earth – i.e. they were to be stewards of the earth's resources

There is a lot of spiritual meat in these verses, but since our focus in on the first marriage, we'll just summarize this overview by saying that God created the human race with a plan, a purpose, and the necessary provision to accomplish these things. We'll start to look at some of the details in Genesis Two.

Genesis 2: Filling in The Details

Genesis chapter one gives us an overview of creation, while chapter two begins to fill in the details. Chronologically, Genesis 2 fits in between various verses of Genesis 1. In looking specifically at the creation of man and woman, we read in chapter one:

> Then God said,"Let Us make man in Our image, according to Our likeness; and let them rule over the fish of the sea and over the birds of the sky and over the cattle and over all the earth and over every creeping thing that creeps on the earth." And God created man in His own image, in the image of God He created him; male and female He created them.
> Gen. 1:26-27

How were they created? In God's image. Much speculation is made about the word "image," also translated "likeness." I can't add anything to that debate, but I was interested in the definition from *Strong's Exhaustive Concordance*.

> Likeness. Strong's #6754, צלם, *tselem* - from an unused root meaning to shade; a phantom, i.e. (fig) illusion, resemblance. Hence, a representative figure, especially an idol.

Remembering that "man," as used in these verses, is a generic term for the human race, we see that God created representatives of Himself in male and female forms. At this point, nothing else distinguishes them.

The other thing we see from these verses is what God expected of them. According to Gen. 1:28,

> *And God blessed them; and God said to them, "Be fruitful and multiply, and fill the earth, and subdue it; and rule.*
> Gen. 1:28a

What were they to do?
1. Be fruitful and multiply – this was also given to all the creatures of the earth
2. Rule over the earth – this was given to mankind alone

In Gen. 2:7-22 we observe a few more details. This passage is a bit longer than I've been quoting previously, so instead of writing it out here, I'll let you refer to your own Bible. Read with a purpose! As you read, ask the text *how* they were created, and make a list of what you observe. Here's mine, listed in the order the events occurred:

1. God formed man (the male) from the earth (v 7)
2. God created the garden for him (v 8)
3. God allowed man to look among all the animals for a suitable companion (v 18-20)
4. God created woman from the man's flesh as his perfect companion (v 21-22)

Why did He create woman out of man's body rather than from the dust of the ground as He did man? Because they are literally of one flesh. Even though the Lord created all the animals from the earth, only woman was of the man's kind.

Gen 2:18 and 20 also use the term "helper suitable" or "help meet" (KJV) to describe woman.

> *Then the Lord God said, "It is not good for the man to be alone; I will make him a helper suitable for him." And out of the ground the Lord God formed every beast of the field and every bird of the sky, and brought them to the man to see*

Genesis 2: Filling in The Details

what he would call them; and whatever the man called a living creature, that was its name. The man gave names to all the cattle, and to the birds of the sky, and to every beast of the field, but for Adam there was not found a helper suitable for him. Gen. 2:18-20

> Helper (help). Strong's #5828, עזר, *ezer* - aid
>
> Suitable (meet). Strong's #5048, נגד, *neged* - in front of, part opposite; specifically a counterpart or mate; corresponding to, parallel to, suitable

Woman was a counterpart to aid man. With what?

1. Being fruitful, multiplying, and filling the earth.
2. Ruling over the earth

These are things man cannot do alone.

Why didn't God create male and female simultaneously? My opinion is based on the verses quoted above, Gen 2:18–20. Adam was naming the animals to see if he could find a suitable companion. God was the observer of Adam's reactions. For some reason, Adam had to see for himself that there was no suitable companion amongst the animals. Woman alone was his equal.

Leaving and Cleaving

There are two more verses in Genesis 2 that we need to examine; verses 23 and 24.

> And the man said,
> "This is now bone of my bones,
> And flesh of my flesh,
> She shall be called Woman
> Because she was taken out of Man"
> For this cause a man shall leave his father and his mother
> and shall cleave to his wife; and they shall become one flesh.
> Gen. 2:23-24

When Adam sees Eve he recognizes that she is the perfect companion whom he couldn't find elsewhere. She is unique among all creation. Because of this ("for this cause," or "therefore" in the King James) man is to leave his parents and cleave to his wife.

> Leave. Strong's #5800, עזב, azab - to loosen, i.e. relinquish, forsake, permit, commit self.
>
> Cleave. Strong's #1692, דבק, dabaq - cling, adhere, keep close to, join to

Why? That they might become one flesh. The word "flesh" (Strong's #1320) can mean physical flesh, but it can also mean a body as a unit. We see this formalized in the marriage ceremony, where a man loosens himself from his parents and commits himself to his wife.

Why is this directed at the man and not the woman? That's a good question, and one which these verses don't answer. Perhaps because men tend to be more task/career oriented and need a reminder that marriage is about relationship. That's complete speculation on my part, but I think it often tends to be true.

The word "one" in Gen. 2:24 is of particular interest for how it is used elsewhere.

> One. Strong's #259, אֶחָד, *echad* - united, single, same

This is the same word that is used of God Himself as the Trinity,

> *Hear, O Israel! The Lord is our God, the Lord is* <u>One</u>*!*
> *Deut. 6:4*

A common illustration of the word *echad* is a bunch of grapes. It is one bunch, or unit, of many individual grapes. This is a very strong theological argument for the Trinity.

It makes sense then, that the marriage unit is used as a picture of Christ and the church.

> *We are members of His body. "For this cause a man shall leave his father and mother and shall cleave to his wife; and the two shall become one flesh." This mystery is great; but I am speaking with reference to Christ and the church.*
> *Eph. 5:30-32*

Does that mean we can apply Paul's description of unity to marriage?

> *Make my joy complete by being of the same mind, maintaining the same love, united in spirit, intent on one purpose.* *Phil. 2:2*

I think so. In fact, I think this verse from Philippians would be a great start to a four part series for pre-marital counseling! For those of you considering marriage, this might be an excellent checklist when you are wondering, "Is this the right one for me?"

For those of us already married, we are probably well aware of the areas in our marriages where we have either unity or disunity. Of course, we have been looking at God's intent for men and women in a perfect, unfallen world. Still, this gives us something to work toward.

It also should help us better understand our role as parents. Hopefully we are not clinging to our children, but are preparing and training them to go out from us to be godly husbands and wives. Hopefully, we are not so emotionally bound to them that we will be unable to release them when the time comes.

In Genesis 2:23-24, then, we see the pattern and the goal for a godly marriage.

Companionship in Marriage

Let's take a look at another interesting word in Gen. 2:18 - alone.

> Then the Lord God said, "It is not good for the man to be <u>alone</u>; I will make him a helper suitable for him." Gen. 2:18

> Alone. Strong's #905, בַּד, *bad* - separation, by implication a part of a body, a branch of a tree. "The core concept is to be separate and isolated. It can also connote the idea of dividing into parts."[1]

The implication in the definition of this word is not one of individualism and independence. Rather, it is of isolation and separation from the completeness of the whole. The whole in this case is man + woman = one.

Now, I'm not trying to beat a dead horse, because hopefully we've already settled this point. But for women who struggle with a sense of inferiority, or for men who assume their own superiority because man was created first and woman was taken from his side, this definition should put things into perspective. The point is that in marriage, neither husband nor wife was meant to stand independent of the other, together they make up a whole.

One thing I realized from studying this word, is that it is not simply the woman who is to be a companion to the man. As two parts of a whole, they are equally companions to one another. And because they are one body, their primary fellowship is to be from one another.

Most of us understand this in an intellectual sense at least. After all, no one gets married because they prefer to be by themselves. As time passes, however, many of us find our marriages drifting apart. The reasons for this are numerous. The question is, "What can we do about it?"

Some of the things which foster companionship are attitudes and behaviors at which we've already looked:

From Eph. 5: 22-30
    Husbands – love, nourish, and cherish their wives
    Wives – submit to and respect their husbands

From 1 Peter 3:1-7
    Husbands – be understanding; honor her as a fellow heir
    Wives – be respectful, submissive, and gentle

And from Titus 2:4
    Wives – love their husbands

For some of us, these things may come easily, for others, not so much. It is especially difficult if we feel that our husbands aren't doing their part. In that case, we may even struggle with hurt, anger, or resentment to the point where we just don't want to be companionable.

To me, the two things that I know I can work on are my attitude and my behavior. I cannot control what others (including my husband) think, do, or say. Nor can I change my circumstances. But I can make a difference. How? In my attitude and behavior. I may not be able to make great strides, but I can take small steps. Below are some of the things I try to do to nurture companionship in my marriage.

∼ Pay attention and listen. It doesn't matter what he's talking about, I try to stop what I'm doing, turn toward him, look him in the eye, and listen without interrupting. I tend to be an interrupter, so this is not always easy for me. If I have something pressing to do (like stirring the gravy so it doesn't scorch), I tell him, "I need to stir the gravy, but I'm interested in what you're saying. I can listen while I do this."

~ *Be encouraging without offering advice.* If he's had a bad day, he just needs to know I'm on his side. Companions don't try to fix one another's lives, they offer sympathetic support. My husband doesn't need for me to tell him what to do or quote Scripture at him. He especially doesn't need for me to point out what he's doing wrong. Believe me, I've done all these things and they definitely don't foster unity between us. If and when he wants my opinion, he'll ask.

~ *Spend time with him.* No one gets married to be alone. Time together doesn't always have to be paying attention to one another, it can also be simply being together. If he wants to watch football or "This Old House" on television, I sit with him, even if I have other things to do. I'm not usually interested in television, so I do handwork. We don't always have to talk; silence can be companionable too.

~ *Develop or encourage common interests.* Most of us are aware that when a couple is in it's child-rearing stage, it is very easy for a wife to be completely focused on the children and their needs. Husbands often focus entirely on developing their jobs or careers. The drifting apart isn't intentional, it is a consequence of each focusing their attention elsewhere. Most of us probably know of at least one couple who found, once the children had grown up and left the nest, that they were as two strangers with nothing in common. The answer to this is to strive to develop or maintain interests in common. This could be anything: reading, hobbies, sports, volunteer work. Whatever you choose, consider it an important investment in your marriage and its future.

∼ Treats for grown-ups only. Many couples have a weekly date night, but sometimes we couldn't afford that. One thing I'd do (when our children were still at home), would be to keep something special around, like my husband's favorite ice cream. I wouldn't even let the kids know I had it. After they went to bed, it was a special secret treat, for just the two of us.

These are things we've worked on in our own marriage, and I can honestly say that we are better friends now than when we first married.

Help Meet

The second chapter of Genesis describes the first woman as a "Help Meet." At least that's the term used in the King James Version. The New American Standard uses "Helper Suitable." Other translations use the term "suitable helper," (NIV); helper meet (suitable, adapted, complementary), (Amplified Bible); "helper fit", (ESV); "helper — as his counterpart" (Young's Literal Translation); "right kind of partner," (CEV). When we looked up the Hebrew in "Genesis 2: Filling in The Details", we saw that "help" meant to aid, and "meet" meant counterpart, corresponding to, or parallel to.

> *Then the Lord God said, "It is not good for the man to be alone; I will make him a <u>helper suitable</u> for him.*   Gen. 2:18

> *The man gave names to all the cattle, and to the birds of the sky, and to every beast of the field, but for Adam there was not found a <u>helper suitable</u> for him.*   Gen. 2:20

We see that the Lord was addressing the man's aloneness. Hence we focused first on companionship. But by using the term "helper suitable," we see that Eve's function was much broader than simply keeping him company. Adam needed help. He could not fulfill God's plan by himself.

Even though this passage never uses the term "companion," it is still a vital concept to understand. Why? Because I think it helps offset the idea that being a helper means merely being some sort of assistant. If we cannot help voluntarily - if we must be compelled like an employee who helps for money, or ordered like a servant or slave - then companionship does not exist and we are alone in our position.

So what happens? On the one hand, men are tempted with spiritual pride by believing they have a God-given superiority, having been created first. Women on the other hand are tempted to rebellion, by believing the lie that equality is based on function (what we do) and ownership (what we have).

Indeed, much of the struggle for women's equality is based on being able to function in society as men do: to have the same kinds of jobs and careers, to climb the same career ladders, to receive the same salary, to be treated in the same manner. On one level, this seems very logical. However, I have made an interesting observation within my own lifetime. I have observed my grandmother's generation, who felt fulfilled in their domestic role; my mother's generation, who were dissatisfied with it; my generation, who fought long and hard for the right to abandon it; and my daughter's generation, who have proudly opted to stay home as mothers and homemakers. Women have confused their sense of personal fulfillment with the sin nature's basic dissatisfaction with life.

The other area in which we judge our sense of equality is in what we have, or our possessions. Indeed, we train our children to be this way. I recall a time when my children were small and I was reading in a parents' magazine about children's birthday parties. The advice given was that the host should make sure that everyone got a present, to make things fair. This struck me as rather sad because it was setting up a precedent of expectation in these children, that their equality was based on having the same thing as everyone else. I preferred to view birthday parties differently, that it was the birthday boy's or girl's turn to get presents. When it was my child's birthday, it was their turn. My children accepted this happily and never complained about unfairness.

If we believe that our equality is based upon doing the same tasks, or having the same possessions as others, we will spend all our lives in frustration. Not only because we cannot ultimately achieve this kind of fairness, but because we were never created to find our fulfillment in these things.

What has all this got to do with being a help meet? I think because the term, "helper" connotes something other than the intended meaning. Yet besides trying to clarify the definition, there is a biblical example we can look to as well. Paul uses the same image of one body in describing the church in 1 Cor 12:12-27. Apparently the Corinthians were quibbling over who was more important.

> *For the body is not one member, but many ... if the whole body were an eye, where would the hearing be? ... it is much truer that the members of the body which seem to be weaker are necessary; and those members of the body which we deem less honorable, on these we bestow more abundant honor ... that there should be no division in the body, but that the members should have the same care for one another.*
>
> 1 Cor 12: 14, 17, 22, 23, 25

How appropriate that God should use marriage as a picture of the church! But what is the solution to divisions? 1 Corinthians 13. Christian love is the key to unity. It is a passage of Scripture which I come back to again and again. It is appropriate for so many instances, not least of all our marriages.

Genesis 3: So What Happened?

> Now the serpent was more crafty than any beast of the field which the Lord God had made. And he said to the woman, "Indeed, has God said, 'You shall not eat from any tree of the garden'?"
> Gen. 3:1

I don't know about you, but the first question that pops into my mind is "why the woman?" Much is made of this fact in teachings about the roles of men and women. What we need to do, however, is to follow the principles of inductive Bible study and see what Scripture says before jumping to any conclusions.

We should note that the serpent misquotes the Lord God by saying "any tree." Of course, since the serpent is crafty, we know this is deliberate. But in looking at Eve's answer, we see that she misquotes as well.

> And the woman said to the serpent, "From the fruit of the trees of the garden we may eat; but from the fruit of the tree which is in the middle of the garden, God has said, 'You shall not eat from it or touch it, lest you die.'"
> Gen. 3:2-3

Eve added "or touch it." We can speculate as to the reason, but the text doesn't give us this information.

Another disturbing fact is found in this verse,

> She took its fruit and ate; and she gave also to her husband with her, and he ate.
> Gen. 3:6b

"With her." Again, questions! Did Adam observe the entire interaction between his wife and the serpent? It doesn't say she took it to her husband. And why did he eat too, knowing that God had said don't? Again, we can only speculate. We do know from chapter two, that the command about the Tree of the Knowledge of Good and Evil, was given to Adam before Eve was created (Gen. 2:15-17). Yet we also know, from what she told the serpent, that she knew of the command as well.

To make matters worse, both Adam and Eve blamed someone else when confronted (Gen. 2:12-13). Adam blamed his wife and Eve blamed the serpent. But she also says something very revealing,

> *Then the Lord God said to the woman, "What have you done?" And the woman said, "The serpent deceived me and I ate."* Gen. 3:13

I'd like to take a closer look at the word, "deceived" next time. For now, we need to understand that there are consequences for disobedience. In Gen. 2: 14-24 God spells out those consequences, which unfortunately didn't only affect Adam and Eve; they have and continue to affect us as well.

The worst of these consequences is the knowledge of good and evil. Now, ordinarily we think of knowledge as being a good thing. One can never have too much information (knowledge), right? But the Hebrew here, *yada*, indicates an intimate knowledge obtained through the senses. It indicates an acquaintance with, or familiarity.

What we see is not a simple knowing about something, as in reading a book about it. We see knowing on a very personal, intimate level based on mental, emotional, and physical experience. And that is one of the saddest consequences of sin; the experience of evil.

We usually think of death as being the consequence for sin and we give thanks to Jesus for releasing us from sin's penalty. Yet between birth and death we experience the

Genesis 3: So What Happened?

knowledge of evil. We live out the consequences of choices made, both our own and those of others. Sadly, one's choices always effect others. Have you ever heard someone say, "It's not hurting anybody" to justify their actions? The problem is that it only looks that way in our finiteness. Eve could well have said the same thing.

Because we have free will, we spend our entire lives making choices. We can choose to be obedient to God's Word, or we can yield to some tempting reason to disobey. It is difficult because obedience truly requires faith. It requires trusting God on an unseen level, one often in contradiction to our thoughts and feelings. Yet so much rides on it.

Next, we'll take a look at "why the woman" and see if we can find anything in Scripture to answer that question.

Deceived

> *Then the Lord God said to the woman, "What have you done?" And the woman said, "The serpent <u>deceived</u> me and I ate."*
> Gen. 3:13

> Deceive. Strong's #5377, נשׁא, nasha' - to lead astray, i.e (mentally) to delude, or (morally) to seduce.

Why the woman? When we start looking at what went wrong in the Garden of Eden, we are eventually faced with this question. It seems reasonable to assume that the serpent chose the most likely target. But what was it about the woman that made her easier to deceive? Scripture doesn't offer a clear-cut answer. In fact, Eve was not tempted any differently than anyone is tempted.

How was that? Compare Gen. 3:6 with 1 John 2:16.

> *When the woman saw that the tree was good for food, and that it was a delight to the eyes, and that the tree was desirable to make one wise, she took its fruit and ate.*
> Gen. 3:6

> *For all that is in the world, the lust of the flesh and the lust of the eyes and the boastful pride of life, is not from the Father, but is from the world.*
> 1 John 2:16

Eve saw that the tree was good for food (the lust of the flesh), it was a delight to the eyes (the lust of the eyes), and it was desirable to make one wise like God (spiritual pride). These are the same ways we're all tempted, including Jesus.

Lust of the flesh:

> He became hungry. And the tempter came and said to him, "If You are the Son of God, command these stones become bread"
> John 4:2b-3

Lust of the eyes:

> Again, the devil ... showed Him all the kingdoms of the world and their glory; and he said to Him, "All these things I will give You, if You fall down and worship me."
> John 2:8-9

Spiritual pride:

> Then the devil took Him into the holy city; and he had Him stand on the pinnacle of the temple, and said to Him, "If you are the Son of God throw Yourself down; for it is written, 'He will give His angels charge concerning You'"
> John 2:5-6a

In addition to believing the devil's voice of temptation, Eve believed the same lie we all believe: "You can get away with it" (Gen. 3:4).

So what was it that made Eve easier to deceive? Based on everything we have studied so far I have an opinion.

It is often said that men are initiators and women are responders. Personally I believe this is true, although I cannot offer a verse or passage in Scripture which clearly states this. I do think it can be inferred from Scripture. This concept is often criticized as being nothing but cultural stereotypes, as though being responsive is a weakness. Yet I think our role as responders is a strength. For one thing, it is necessary for nurturing our children. For another, it gives us a mental and emotional flexibility which, aside from our rebellious sinful natures, enables us to submit to our husbands more easily than they are able to submit to their authority. On the other hand, it can be exploited by others.

> For among them are those who enter into households and captivate weak women. 2 Tim. 3:6

Now, without chasing a rabbit down a rabbit trail, I would like to ask you ladies a question. Have you ever been approached by a man who wants you to ask or convince your husband to do something? He has an excellent argument for what he wants, so that you agree to speak with your husband about it. But have you asked yourself why this man is coming to you about it rather than going directly to your husband? If 2 Timothy 3:6 is true, then it may be because such a man thinks the woman will be easier to influence in order to get what he wants.

Since it is in our natures to respond to the needs of others, care must be taken that we are not taken advantage of. I think that this is why the serpent chose Eve as his target. I think it is also why the husband was given the responsibility to spiritually protect his wife.

> Husbands, love your wives just as Christ also loved the church and gave Himself up for her; that He might sanctify her, having cleansed her by the washing of the water with the word, that He might present to Himself the church in all her glory, having no spot or wrinkle or any such thing; but that she should be holy and blameless. Eph. 5:25-27

I think it is another reason why the wife is to submit to the husband rather than the other way around - to protect her from a multitude of influences to which she may be inclined to respond. Her husband is to serve as a filter, to protect his wife's spiritual purity.

Together husband and wife are to pray and seek the Lord. In a perfect world, they would function in perfect harmony and fulfill God's plan for their lives. There would not be a need for an imposed authority structure. Yet even in a perfect world man and woman wanted to go their own way. Yes, Eve was deceived, but Adam was willfully disobedient. Neither action paints a very flattering picture for anyone.

In the end, the whys and wherefores don't impact the outcome. We may feel better about understanding, but unless we are willing to trust the Lord now, and be obedient to His Word now, then we are in the same boat as the first man and woman: either deceived or willfully disobedient. I encourage you to be neither. I encourage you to trust the Lord even when you don't understand. I encourage you to take Him at His word even when it doesn't seem to make sense. Why?

> *And without faith it is impossible to please Him.*
> Heb. 11:6

Let us make it our goal to always please Him.

The Consequences

Disobedience changes things. In Genesis chapters one and two, we saw that the Creator had a plan for His creation. When Adam and Eve stepped outside of this plan, all of creation was set on a different course.

We've already seen that one major consequence of their disobedience was the experiential knowledge of evil. But there were other consequences as well, individual consequences for the serpent, man, and woman. We're going to focus on the consequences for the woman.

> To the woman He said,
> "I will greatly multiply
> Your pain in childbirth,
> In pain you shall bring forth children;
> Yet your desire shall be for your husband,
> And he shall rule over you."
>
> Gen. 3:16

The first consequence was pain in childbirth. The King James Version uses the word "sorrow." Interestingly, two different Hebrew words were originally used in this verse, although they come from the same root.

> Pain. Strong's #6087, עצב, atsab - worry, pain, anger. According to TWOT[1], it refers to both physical pain as well as emotional sorrow.

What does that mean? The obvious thing is the physical pain of childbirth itself. It can be horrific. However, this pain usually does not overshadow the joy of the new baby itself. If it didn't, women would probably stop having children!

But what of the emotional sorrow? I think that comes later, when children begin to experience for themselves the consequences of living in a fallen world. Most mothers would do anything to protect their children from pain, fear, rejection, failure, humiliation, prejudice, unfair treatment, etc. Of course, this is something we cannot do, which is why parents are instructed to train their children in godliness. We cannot insulate them from the consequences of living in a fallen world, but we can teach them how to live in that fallen world.

That emotional sorrow occurs as our children begin to make their own choices, often unwise, and often with disastrous results. This is why we have such verses in Proverbs as:

> *A wise son makes a father glad, but a foolish son is a grief to his mother.*   Prov. 10:1

> *A foolish son is a grief to his father and bitterness to her who bore him.*   Prov. 17:25

It is also why we get controversial verses such as:

> *He who withholds his rod hates his son, but he who loves him disciplines him diligently.*   Prov. 13:24

> *Discipline your son while there is hope, and do not desire his death.*   Prov. 19:18

> *Foolishness is bound up in the heart of a child; the rod of discipline will remove it far from him.*   Prov. 22:15

> *Correct your son, and he will give you comfort; he will also delight your soul.*   Prov. 29:17

The Consequences

Having a sin nature means being naturally self-centered. It means wanting our own way. Children do not have to be taught to be selfish; this is a natural part of the fallen human nature. If left unchecked, selfishness will grow into self-indulgence without regard for the consequences to either self or others. Such people make very foolish choices regarding their lives based on short term self-gratification rather than the long term results of such decisions or long term goals for something better. It is cruel to allow a child to grow up this way.

These verses in Proverbs recognize that human nature does not change without motivation. We may change our behavior to obtain something favorable, or we may change it to escape something unfavorable. Knowledge does not change human behavior; consequences change behavior. For example, it isn't the knowledge of cancer which usually motivates people to stop smoking and eat their green, leafy vegetables. It is having cancer which more likely brings about these changes.

If we recognize that babies are born with a sin nature, then we understand the need to equip them to minimize its consequences. It would be wonderful if we could impart our experience another way, but in the end, what is needed is training in self-discipline and self-control. Proverbs simply states that the brief sting of the rod is small when compared to the greater injury that an undisciplined, reckless life can bring. We may or may not choose to use the rod, but the seriousness of the consequences of a child's foolish choices is no less severe.

As parents we are always relieved when our children make wise choices. To see them make wrong or foolish choices is painful indeed. Yet according to Gen. 3:16, it is a consequence of our fallen nature.

Besides pain in childbirth, another consequence for Eve's disobedience is an externally imposed order on marriage. Husband and wife were created of one flesh, intended to be two complimentary parts of a whole. Being perfect, they would function exactly as the Lord intended, fulfilling the purpose for which they were created. Sin destroyed the natural unity and harmony which were meant to exist between husband and wife. No longer would they instinctively work together, now they would strive against one another and compete with one another.

To preserve the marital and family unit, order had to be established. Woman was now placed under the rule of her husband (Gen. 3:16).

> Rule. Strong's #4910, מָשַׁל, *mashal* - to rule, have dominion, reign

Why the woman? Because she was disobedient. Whether she was deceived or not, she knew that they were not supposed to eat the fruit of the Tree of the Knowledge of Good and Evil, and she knew that there would be consequences for disobeying (Gen. 3:2-3). Yet she did it anyway. We may well try to argue that we shouldn't suffer the consequences of her sin, yet that is the problem with sin. Its consequences affect everything. It is not only the sinner who suffers those consequences, but untold others as well. The argument "it isn't hurting anybody" is an illusion.

We might well wish to point out that Adam was disobedient as well, so why was his wife put under him? Why not him under her? First of all, because she sinned first. But before we begin to resent Adam, we need to remember that Man has his own set of consequences. These may look less stringent than those given to Woman, but they are, in fact, no better at all. Adam's consequences for sin do not put men in a more enviable position: toil, thorns, thistles, and sweat just to a decent meal (Gen. 3:17-19). Does hot, sticky, back-breaking work in the swealting summer sun, or freezing, bone-chilling labor in the icy, frigid winter really sound more desirable than working in the comfort of one's own home?

The other consequence mentioned in Gen. 3:16 for the woman is, "Yet your desire shall be for your husband."

> Desire. Strong's #8669, תְּשׁוּקָה, *teshuwqah* - in the original sense of stretching out after, a longing.

This word is used only three times in the Old Testament. Here in Gen. 3:16, in Song of Solomon 7:10, (describing the Beloved's desire for his bride), and in Gen. 4:7, (when the Lord tells Cain that sin desires to rule over him).

I have heard it taught that some biblical scholars interpret desire to mean "to devour" and therefore refers to a woman's desire to dominate her husband. I cannot find this by doing my own word studies. I can find that this is one of the meanings when used in the context of animals, but unless one is willing to classify women as mere animals (which negates everything the Lord said), then it is quite a quantum leap in biblical interpretation.

What I do see, is that women have a deep-seated desire to be married. No matter how liberated she becomes, no matter how career oriented she is, she still has the desire for a husband and children. And this seems to be the case throughout history and across all cultures. Sometimes women struggle against that desire. I have met women who claim that they never wished to marry, but conversation will usually turn up a deep hurt from the past. Another example is the booming wedding industry which capitalizes on this desire.

We cannot change the consequences of sin. The question therefore becomes, how do we choose to live our lives in spite of it? We can balk and complain. We can look for philosophical loopholes. We can shake our fists at God and say, "It's not fair." We can fight and strive to make things different. But in the end we can change very little. Except our attitudes.

Sometimes I am victorious in this area, sometimes I am not. When I am not, there are some verses that I cling to. I would like to close by sharing them with you.

> *Humble yourselves therefore under the mighty hand of God, that He may exalt you at the proper time, casting all your cares upon Him because He cares for you... And after you have suffered for a little while, the God of all grace, who called you to His eternal glory in Christ, will Himself perfect, confirm, strengthen, and establish you.*
>
> 1 Peter 5: 6, 7, 10

---

[1]*Theological Wordbook of the Old Testament*, Laird, Archer, & Waltke, (Moody Press, Chicago, 1980) Vol I. 687

The Problem With Sin

The true temptation of Eve was to trust her own judgment rather than the Lord God's. She listened to someone other than God and was deceived into thinking that her judgment was better than His. She believed that God was depriving her of something; and although Adam knew better (1 Tim. 2:14), he chose to follow Eve. Their actions changed human nature.

Unfortunately the consequences for disobedience apply to us too, and we can't change them. So how are we to live in spite of them? I think that first we need to get to the bottom line, which is sin. Sin is the common thread throughout history which unites us with that first couple in that first marriage.

The problem with sin is that it replaces God with Self. It replaces trust in Him with trusting our own judgment. We do what we want to do because sin deceives us into believing that we are wiser than God, that we know better than God. And if we are wiser than God, then we are wiser than others, we know better than others.

Most of the conflict we experience in marriage is because we each want our own way. We each think we know better than the other, and so we argue and fight over money, children, in-laws, jobs, habits, friends, pastimes, church, etc. Even if the issues are valid ones, it's the demanding of our own way that is the problem.

So what can we do about it? The world says we need to fight for our rights. The Bible says we are to lay them down and serve others. Jesus' example for us was to perform the most menial service to His disciples by washing their feet (John 13:14).

Paul worded it like this:

> *Do nothing from selfishness or empty conceit, but with humility of mind let each of you regard one another as more important than himself; do not merely look out for your own personal interests, but also for the interests of others. Have this attitude in yourselves which was also in Christ Jesus, who, although He existed in the form of God, did not regard equality with God a thing to be grasped, but emptied Himself, taking the form of a bond-servant, and being made in the likeness of men.*
>
> Phil. 2:3-7

Like Eve, our problem is in trusting our own judgment and following our own desires. And like Eve, our actions have consequences which effect not only ourselves but others as well. Fortunately, God Himself came to show us another way. It is only when we turn from Self and follow Him that we find that the only thing we have been deprived of, is an illusion of freedom.

Being a Godly Woman

My husband and I joke sometimes about how long the line will be in heaven to ask Adam and Eve, "Why did you do it?" I'm sure every believer wonders about that at some time or another. However, if Adam and Eve hadn't been disobedient, someone else certainly would have, and we'd still live in a fallen world today no matter who sinned first.

Sometimes when I am challenged by unbelievers as to why God allows horrible things to happen in the world, I say, "Oh, He could fix it easily. All He would have to do is take away everyone's free will." I'm not trying to be facetious with this answer, I'm just trying to point out that the world's problems aren't God's fault; they are the result of our sinful choices. The question for us as Christians is not how can we fix the consequences of sin, but how we live in spite of them. How do we live in a sinful world, without participating in sin? How do we live our lives according to God's will and His plan for us as individuals and as a people? For anyone who tries to do this, we know it isn't easy. Mankind seems to have lost the way.

When we come to Christ, we are given a new beginning. Not that the circumstances of our lives change, but we change. With that change is an opportunity to live our lives differently, to live them according to the plan God has for us. Not that we automatically stop wanting to sin, but in Christ, we now have the freedom to choose to not sin.

This isn't easy for a couple of reasons. First, we still have the flesh to deal with, which constantly demands its own way. Also the world pressures us with its own definitions of who women are and what we are supposed to do. All of this is in opposition to the Word of God.

So how can we be godly women? I think it's important to study passages such as Titus 2:3-5, but also I think it is helpful to take a look at some of the women of the Bible. Not everyone in the Bible is an example of godly living, but one woman in particular has become my heroine - the Proverbs 31 Woman. In the next chapter I want to begin to look at this passage of Scripture, in hopes that we can see a role model for today's Christian woman as well.

Proverbs 31:10-31

The Excellent Woman: By Whose Definition?

I'd like to begin our study of the Proverbs 31 woman by asking you to read the entire chapter. This will put our target verses in context. As we read, we observe the text by asking it questions: who, what, where, when, why, and how? One of the first things we look for is the author and recipient and what we can learn about them.

The Book of Proverbs is credited to King Solomon (Prov. 1:1). Chapter 31 however, begins with this verse,

> The words of King Lemuel, the oracle which his mother taught him.   Prov. 31:1

This should raise a lot of questions. Who is King Lemuel? Who is his mother? How much of chapter 31 is the oracle - all of it, or only verses 1 – 9, as they are in the English Bible? While we may not know for certain, we can develop some educated opinions.

Who is King Lemuel? Evidently the rabbis believed him to be Solomon. Many Christian Bible scholars agree with this, but others think he is someone different. Since we know that Solomon authored the rest of Proverbs, we may well wonder why he would record someone else's words, especially since Lemuel was never a king of Israel, and since Solomon had his own wisdom. Perhaps it was added later? It seems to make more sense that Solomon is Lemuel, rather than the alternatives. Why he chose this pseudonym is unknown as well.

Who is his mother? If Solomon is the author, then Bathsheba is his mother. (2 Samuel 12:24)

How much of chapter 31 is the oracle? Is it the first nine verses or the entire chapter? Many Bible commentaries limit her advice to the first nine verses. However, the Hebrew Bible doesn't have paragraph divisions, so the paragraphs aren't solid evidence on which to base an opinion. Why is this even of importance? In some ways it's not. But I am personally curious as to whether the Proverbs 31 woman is a woman's idea of an ideal wife, or a man's. It would be interesting to ask various men and women to describe the qualities of a perfect wife. I may be wrong, but I suspect the Proverbs 31 woman would fit women's descriptions more than men's.

The word oracle is interesting to look at. It is translated prophecy in the King James.

> Oracle. Strong's #4853, מַשָּׂא, *massa'* - burden, load, tribute, that which is carried or borne; figuratively an utterance, oracle.

Obviously King Lemuel's mother had a real burden about some things in her son's life: that he not allow himself to be destroyed by drunkenness (v. 4 – 7), nor women (v. 3), that he protect the rights of the needy (v. 8, 9) and especially as to the type of woman he should marry (V. 10 – 31). Starting in chapter four, Solomon had recorded the instructions his father had given him. It makes sense that now in chapter 31, he lastly recorded the advice from his mother.

Next, we'll start taking a look at what she had to say about an excellent wife.

A Woman's Power

An excellent wife, who can find?
For her worth is far above jewels.
                                        Prov. 31:10

In reading through Proverbs 31:10-31, we see a list of qualities which qualify this woman for the description of excellent. I propose to look at these qualities verse by verse, and lastly summarize them. Beginning with verse ten, my first question is, "What does it mean to be excellent?"

> Excellent. Strong's #2428, חיל, *chayil* - a force, whether of men, means, or other resources. To be firm, or strong. An army, wealth, virtue, valor, might, strength, power.

In other words, an excellent woman is a force to be reckoned with. This makes sense, considering that she is to be a guardian of her household. This is also a far cry from the idea that the Bible portrays women as the inferior, weak-willed property of men. But we need to understand something else. When we look at the context of the Proverbs 31 Woman, we see that she is united with her husband, not in competition with him. There is no strife or conflict between husband and wife. How do we know?

The heart of her husband trusts in her.   Prov. 31:11a

She does not use her power to try to dominate her husband, nor does she use it to undermine him, nor to get her own way. Rather, she uses it to protect, nurture, and structure her household. What we see is an example of the pattern for marriage that we saw in Genesis 2: unity, companionship, and teamwork. Verse ten concludes:

For her worth is far above jewels.   Prov. 31:10

In other words, no amount of money can compare to such a wife. A man is better off with such a wife than with wealth. Such a woman is not to be feared, but sought after.

I don't know about you, but I certainly want to be an excellent woman. We'll take the verses which follow one by one, and study the qualites that earn a woman the description of excellent.

A Husband's Trust

The heart of her husband trusts in her,
And he will have no lack of gain.
                                       Prov. 31:11

For a verse that is easy to overlook, this one says a lot. No, it doesn't say anything about the Excellent Woman directly, but her husband's response to her is a reflection on her character as well as their relationship.

I'd like to start by looking up two words in this verse:

> Heart. Strong's #3820, לב, *leb* - the heart; figuratively used widely for the feelings, the will, and even the intellect. Also translated mind, understanding, wisdom.
>
> Trust. Strong's #982, בטח, *batach* - to hasten toward refuge; figuratively to trust, be confident, be secure in, be sure. The KJV says "doth safely trust in her."

What do we see? A woman who evokes her husband's complete confidence in her, not only in the way she manages their home and raises their children, but in their relationship as well. She doesn't use her strengths and abilities to compete with him, but to strengthen unity between them.

What does she do specifically to possess this trust? Scripture gives a few details:

> *And he will have no lack of gain.*   Prov. 31:11b

Verse eleven tells us he has no lack of gain. The KJV words it, "He shall have no need of spoil." I'm not sure if this is because together, they have accumulated enough wealth to have financial security, or because of how well she manages their money, or because he's so content with their relationship that he has no desire to chase after anything else. At the very least we see that he is content with their lifestyle as well as their marriage.

> *She does him good and not evil*
> *All the days of her life.*
> *Prov. 31:12*

Good. Strong's #2896, טוֹב, *towb* - kind, benign, pleasant, agreeable, benefit, welfare

Evil. Strong's #7451, רַע, *ra* - bad, calamity, misery, distress, injury

In other words, she is not simply nice to him, but she always ("all the days of her life") has his best interests at heart. She doesn't seek to hurt him or undermine him; rather, she keeps his welfare in mind and seeks to benefit him.

What we see in their marriage is a fulfillment of God's original intention for marriage: unity. We also see an example of what it means to be a godly Help Meet.

Time for prayerful reflection:

~ Do I always have my husband's needs in mind?

~ Do I have his best interests at heart?

~ Is our home a refuge for him?

A Husband's Trust

~ Do I take council with my husband before making decisions?

~ Do I follow his advice?

~ Do I insist on doing everything my own way?

~ Do I do things behind his back?

~ Do I keep secrets from him?

~ Am I trying to change him?

~ Do I feel that all the problems in our marriage are because of him?

~ Do I complain about him behind his back?

~ Do I feel I have to correct him?

~ Do I continually have to prove I'm right?

~ What am I doing to nurture trust between us?

Unfortunately, once trust is broken, it is nearly impossible to mend.

> *A brother offended is harder to be won than a strong city.*
> Prov. 18:19

Fortunately, it is not impossible.

> *For nothing will be impossible with God.* Luke 1:37

If we want to work on improving our marriages, gaining and keeping our husband's trust would be a good place to start. If trust has been broken in your marriage, the place to begin is with repentance and asking your husband for his forgiveness. The next step is to begin to bring forth fruit in keeping with repentance. (Matt. 3:8)

Some of us may have to work hard at it, but we can count on the Lord's grace as we take our first steps toward living out His word.

Willingly Industrious

She looks for wool and flax,
And works with her hands in delight.
                              Prov. 31:13

At first glance, this verse might seem irrelevant for modern women. Thanks to the industrial revolution, raw wool and flax are two things we never need to bother with. In fact, we really may not know too much about them.

Most of us probably know that wool comes from sheep. Flax, however, we mostly hear of in reference to flax seed as a health food supplement. From that we can guess that it is a plant. However, it has another purpose as well - linen is made from it. Wool and flax should speak to us of fabric.

Our homes are filled with fabrics: clothing, upholstery, curtains and draperies, table linens, towels, even our carpeting is made from yarn. It is with fabrics that a large part of interior decoration is made, using color and texture to create an atmosphere in which we feel comfortable. Fabrics also make clothing, which have both functional as well as decorative uses.

From this verse I think that we get a glimpse of the Proverbs 31 Woman as a homemaker. She is domestically inclined and we see that her home is a priority. She obviously doesn't do it because they can't afford to purchase ready-made fabrics, but because she loves doing it.

She works with her hands in delight.   Prov. 31:13b

> Works. Strong's #6213, עשה, asah - to do, make, produce, fashion, accomplish, make, be busy, be industrious

> Delight. Strong's #2656, חפץ, *chephets* - Delight, pleasure, that in which one takes delight. Also translated acceptable, desire, things desired, matter, pleasant, pleasure, purpose, willingly.

From this (and the verses which follow) we can see that she is willingly industrious. She enjoys working with her hands and seeks out the raw materials, even though (as we will see) she is wealthy enough to afford to purchase ready-made items from the merchants.

How does that apply to us? Few of us are going to start from scratch to make first the yarn, then the fabrics, then sew the items ourselves. However, we can glean a few things from this verse.

One thing we see is that she is not idle. Nor does she view her life as a homemaker as boring and unfulfilling. Rather, her home and family are a creative outlet for her. Now, you may or may not enjoy or know how to sew. Perhaps more to the point is our attitudes toward our homes, and how seriously we take our spiritual responsibility toward them. As Guardians of the Home, we have a responsibility to create and protect a welcoming and nurturing environment within our homes: for our husbands, our children, our guests, and ourselves. We also have the responsibility to make sure our family is appropriately clothed. Not that we should be slaves to fashion, but because as Christians, we represent our Lord and the life of the Redeemed.

The Proverbs 31 Woman is willingly industrious in these matters. As we continue to study her and her character, we hopefully will see this more clearly.

Diligent Provider

She is like merchant ships;
She brings her food from afar.
                    Prov. 31:14

I used to read this verse and think, "Okay, so she does the grocery shopping." Writing about this verse, however, has forced me to meditate on it. One thing we should notice is the word "like," because it signals a comparison. What does the comparison to merchant ships show us about the Proverbs 31 Woman?

> Merchant. Strong's #5503, סחר, *cachar* - to go around, go about, travel about, go about in trade

So too, the Proverbs 31 Woman is willing to go out and seek after choice ingredients for her family's meals. In other words, she doesn't simply do the quickest, easiest thing: fast food take-out or microwaveable meals. Rather, she is diligent to provide good food for her family.

This verse companioned with the previous verse,

> *She looks for wool and flax,*
> *And works with her hands in delight.*
>   Prov. 31:13

gives us the domestic arts in a nutshell. From them, we see that the Excellent Wife is domestically inclined in both the textile and culinary arts. Not only that, but she is personally involved in the process, from fabric making to menu planning and food selection for her family. Although wealthy, she is not merely an overseer, hiring someone to do all these things for her; rather, she does them herself.

One modern objection to homemaking is that it is unfulfilling. Today's women are often convinced that they will be bored if they stay at home. Consequently, they seek stimulation and fulfillment elsewhere. For some women it is with a job or career. For others, it is church ministry. Is there anything wrong with these things? From the verses which follow, we will see that the Proverbs 31 Woman herself had both. Nowhere, however, can we conclude that her outside activities were motivated by a sense of boredom or unfullfillment. Nor did she neglect her domestic responsibilities.

> *She looks well to the ways of her household, and does not eat the bread of idleness. Her children rise up and bless her; Her husband also, and he praises her.*   Prov. 31:27-28

This is something to consider as we make choices for our lives and set our priorities. Which would mean more to you? A brief acknowledgement by your boss for a job well done? Your name mentioned occasionally in the church bulletin for ministry participation? Or the praises and blessings of your family for the love and care you've demonstrated toward them over the years?

We all make daily choices about what we will do and how we will do it. I exhort you, Christian Women, to be true Keepers (Guardians) of your homes in the choices you make. Although it may not seem rewarding at present, at the very least, you are storing up treasures in heaven. You will not go unrewarded for your sacrifice.

Organized Manager

She rises also while it is still night,
And gives food to her household
And portions to her maidens.

Prov. 31:15

I've heard more than one Christian homemaker joke that this early rising business is what keeps her from becoming a truly excellent wife. I have often felt the same way. It would be nice to think that this is just part of the Excellent Woman's personality, yet when we consider how busy she is, we have to admit that rising early is the only way to accomplish so much. But, does the Proverbs 31 Woman drag herself out of bed every morning? Apparently not.

> Rises. Strong's #6965, קוּם, *quwm* - to arise, to stand, to be set, to fulfill, to establish, to endure, to stir up, to carry out. Often used with a sense of rising in preparation or rising in power.

Quwm does not refer to getting out of bed, which is an entirely different word in Hebrew (*shakam*). It refers to rising up with a plan and a purpose. This is what we see the Excellent Woman doing.

The first two items on her daily agenda are to feed her household and attend to her maidens.

1. *Gives food to her household* — We've already seen in verse 14 that she is diligent in selecting and purchasing choice foods for her household. Here we see that she supervises the meals as well. Does she cook them herself? The verse doesn't tell us that. What we do see is that she personally attends to all aspects of feeding her family.

2. *Gives portions to her maidens* — Two words are of interest here: portions and maidens.

> Portions. Strong's #2706, חק, *choq* - an appointment of time, space, quantity, labor or usage. Commandment, custom, decree, prescribed task
>
> Maiden. Strong's #5291, נערה, *na`arah* - girl (from infancy through adolescence), young woman, marriageable young woman, maid, female attendant, female servant

Are these young women her daughters or her servants? *Na`arah* can be used either way. Because the Excellent Woman and her husband are obviously well off, it is highly likely that these are maid servants, who are being given their work assignments for the day. If some or all are daughters, then we see the Excellent Woman training them to become managers of their own homes when they marry.

Either way, we see that the Excellent Woman has a plan before the day begins. She is aware of the needs of the household, and is organized in addressing them. As we see in verse 27,

> *She looks well to the ways of her household,*
> *And does not eat the bread of idleness.*
>
> Prov. 31:27

The fruit of being organized is abundant. Not only are her husband and children happy (verse 28), but in addition to running her household well (verse 27), she has time to run a home business (verse 24), as well as have a ministry to the poor (verse 20).

Time for reflection.

I'll be the first to admit that this is not me. I do rise early to do my Bible study, but at the end of the day I can count the ways that I have frittered away my time. Now that my children have left the nest, I find that I am more relaxed in my approach to housework and meal preparation, so that some things get neglected. In other words, I need to heed this lesson!

How about you?

Shrewd Investor

She considers a field and buys it;
From her earnings she plants a vineyard.
                              Prov. 31:16

> Considers. Strong's #3754, זמם, kerem - thinks about, devises, plans, considers, purposes

This definition confirms something we saw about the Excellent Woman in the last verse we studied.

> *She rises also while it is still night.*   Prov. 31:15a

We saw that "rises" is another word which connotes having a plan and a purpose. From these two verses we might very well conclude that the Excellent Woman is not one who relies on impulse and serendipity to determine the course of her life. Rather, she knows exactly what she is doing and why she is doing it.

From her earnings – This is actually a two part phrase in the Hebrew, translated "with the fruit of her hands" in the King James Version.

> Fruit. Strong's #6529, פרי, perïy - fruit (literally or figuratively): fruit of the ground (produce); fruit of the womb (offspring); or figuratively, fruit of one's actions.

> Hands. Strong's #3709, כף, kaph - the hollow hand or palm; figuratively, power.

I like the idea of "the hollow hand." It gives an image of starting with nothing, as something hollow is empty. The Excellent Woman doesn't take from others to benefit her own plans; rather she relies on her own abilities. And how does she manage that? From the household accounts? With a loan? Rather, from her own earnings. It confirms that she is industrious.

In verse 15, we saw that she managed her household in a well-planned, organized fashion. Here, we see how she manages her money. She has her own earnings which she carefully considers how to spend. She does not use it wastefully or frivolously. She does not use it on fleeting pleasures, or things that can be used up or depreciate in value. Rather, she purchases something with the potential to give her a return - a field in which she can plant a vineyard.

Does this mean her purchase is a business venture? Perhaps, but not necessarily. The purpose of the vineyard may be to supply to her own household. The passage doesn't tell us either way.

She senses that her gain is good.   Prov. 31:18a

In other words, she knows she has made good decisions and has no regrets about them. She doesn't look back and admonish herself for wasteful or imprudent spending. Rather, she invests her money wisely.

Can we say the same? As we look at how we manage our own money or the household accounts, can we say that we feel good about it? One clue may be the temptation to complain that we don't have enough money, that if we only had more we could manage better. It may well be true that we are on tight budgets, but we still have a responsibility to wisely manage what the Lord has allotted us. On the other hand, if we are financially well off, are we guilty of being frivolous and indulgent with our money?

Shrewd Investor

The Excellent Woman used her money wisely, as a tool. This is a goal all Christian women would be wise to work toward, too.

Woman of Strength

She girds herself with strength,
And makes her arms strong.
                                    Prov. 31:17

At first reading, this appears to say that the Excellent Woman works out and is physically fit. This may very well be true, but in doing word studies, we see that the words imply so much more.

> Gird. Strong's #2296. חגר, *chagar* - to bind on, gird oneself, put on a belt
>
> Herself ("loins" in the KJV). Strong's #4974, מתן, *mothen* - From an unused root meaning to be slender; properly the waist or small of the back; only in plural the "loins" or "hips".
>
> Strength. Strong's #5759, עוז or עז, *oze* - boldness, loud, might, power, strength, strong. Can refer to material, physical, social, or political strength.
>
> Arms. Strong's #2220, זרעה or זרו, *zerowa* - arm (literally or as a symbol of strength), forearm, shoulder (of animal sacrificed), strength, force (political and military)
>
> Makes ... strong. Strong's #553, אמץ, '*amats* - To be alert, physically (on foot) or mentally (in courage). To be strong, courageous, brave, stout, bold, solid, hard. In Prov. 31:17, it means to strengthen, secure (for oneself), harden (heart), make firm, make obstinate, assure

From these definitions we see two things. One is that her strength is a physical strength. The other is that she is the one taking action, i.e. her strength is not something that has been bestowed upon her.

I was curious as to what the various commentaries had to say about this verse, so I spent quite a bit of time looking at online resources. Many commentators of Proverbs 31 didn't address this verse specifically, and some applied it to the church as the bride of Christ. The most interesting comment was a footnote to "girds herself with strength" at NETBible.org: "The idea is that of gathering up the long robes with a sash or belt so that they do not get in the way of the work. The point of the figure is readiness for work. But to say she girds herself with 'strength' means that she begins vigorously."[1]

In context we see verse 17 as part of a description of the characteristics of an Excellent Wife. We've already seen that she is industrious, diligent, organized, powerful, trustworthy, and wise. Now we can add strong. Is it merely physical strength? Probably not. Why do I say that? Because it is not physical strength or power which makes an individual excellent; it is what they do with it.

Jesus said (Matt. 6:24) we can serve only one master. Each one of us must decide who that master will be. For the unsaved, there is little choice: they serve themselves, money, or power. As believers, we are free from slavery to sin, so we do have a choice. We can either serve ourselves, or we can serve God. We can use our abilities to become strong and accumulate power for our own gain, or we can use them to serve Christ by serving others.

I'm not talking of serving by giving money to the church or charity. I'm talking about what we do with our time, energy, and influence. People always have time and money for what's important to them. Of the Proverbs 31 Woman we see someone who takes her ministry to her home and family seriously. In addition she helps the poor and needy (verse 20). Her motive?

> *A woman who fears the Lord, she shall be praised.*
> Prov. 31:30b

The Excellent Woman is not excellent because she has accumulated power for herself or because she is so capable. She is excellent because she serves the Lord. Proverbs 31:10-31 is a description of how she does that.

---

[1] NET Bible. https://net.bible.org/#!bible/Proverbs+31

Financially Sensible

What does money mean to you? It is an important question to consider, because money is a fact of life. In studying the example of the Excellent Woman, we have already seen that she is diligent and industrious enough to have money to invest. The next verse gives us the opportunity to consider her attitude towards her wealth as well.

> *She senses that her gain is good;*
> *Her lamp does not go out at night.*
> Prov. 31:18

This verse seems fairly self-explanatory, but just to make sure there isn't possible figurative language here, let's check a couple of definitions.

> Gain. Strong's #5504, סחר, *sachar* - gain, profit, gain from merchandise, gain from traffic
>
> Good. Strong's #2896, טוב, *towb* - good, pleasant, agreeable, excellent

The definitions plus the context -

> *She girds herself with strength,*
> *And makes her arms strong.*
> *She considers a field and buys it;*
> *From her earnings she plants a vineyard.*
> *She senses that her gain is good;*
> *Her lamp does not go out at night.*
> Prov. 31:16 – 18

- confirm that the text is speaking of financial gain.

Over the centuries Christians have run the philosophical gamut concerning the possession of money and wealth. Some view money and material wealth as a hindrance, for example, monastic groups who take vows of poverty. Others view it as proof positive of God's blessing.

Consider Jesus and the Rich Young Ruler (Matt. 19:16-22; Mark 10:17-22; Luke 18-18-23). This young man wanted to know how to obtain eternal life. Their conversation is interesting, because the young man obviously understood that keeping the law wasn't enough. It is from Jesus' response, however, that we begin to gain a spiritual perspective.

> *Looking at him, Jesus felt a love for him and said to him, "One thing you lack: go and sell all you possess and give to the poor, and you will have treasure in heaven; and come, follow Me." But at these words he was saddened, and he went away grieving, for he was one who owned much property.* Mark 10:21-22

Was Jesus saying that money is evil? Was He saying that the rich cannot inherit eternal life?

Jesus also said,

> *No one can serve two masters; for either he will hate the one and love the other, or he will be devoted to one and despise the other. You cannot serve God and wealth.* Matt. 6:24

The question is not whether financial and material wealth is either evil or a blessing. The question is, "Do you own your wealth, or does it own you?"

Have you ever heard someone say, "money is the root of all evil"? That is a misquote. The verse actually says,

> *For the <u>love of money</u> is a root of all sorts of evil, and some by longing for it have wandered away from the faith and pierced themselves with many griefs.* 1 Tim. 6:10

We desire what we love, and we pursue what we desire. So, what does money mean to you? Does it mean material gain? Importance? Power? Security? Freedom? If any of these things ring true for us, then we are in the same boat as the Rich Young Ruler; our desire for wealth is a spiritual stumbling block.

The problem isn't the money, the problem is ownership. As Christians we like to say that everything we own belongs to God, but if we cannot give freely of our material wealth, then our treasure is not in heaven.

So what should our attitude toward money be? One of stewardship. Money is a tool, so how does the Excellent Woman use it?

> *She senses that her gain is good;*
> *Her lamp does not go out at night.*
> Prov. 31:18

We can discover that by examining the other verses in chapter 31 and making a list. We see that:

1. She invests it.

> *She considers a field and buys it;*
> *From her earnings she plants a vineyard.*
> Prov. 31:16

The Proverbs 31 Woman is careful and prudent with her money. Like the good and faithful servants in the parable of the talents (Matt. 15:14-30), she does not hoard it, but she has something to show for her stewardship of it.

2. She uses it for the ministry of her home and family.

> *She looks well to the ways of her household*
> *And does not eat the bread of idleness.*
> *Prov. 31:27*

She is diligent in both feeding (verse 14 and verse 15), and clothing them (verse 13, at which we've already looked, and also verses 19 – 22, at which we'll look soon.)

3. She uses it for ministry to the poor.

> *She extends her hand to the poor;*
> *And she stretches out her hands to the needy.*
> *Prov. 31:20*

We see compassion and generosity here. She uses her hard earned resources to help others.

4. She uses it to be prepared.

> *Her lamp does not go out at night.* Prov. 31:18b

Remember the parable of the prudent and foolish virgins (Matt 25:1-13)? In it, Jesus used a very practical example to illustrate spiritual preparedness. Ten young maidens were waiting for the Bridegroom. Five brought extra oil for their lamps, five didn't. Only the ones with extra oil were prepared to go out and meet the Bridegroom when He arrived at midnight.

We would do well to heed Jesus's point. We live in an age where materialism and affluence (or lack of it) can easily distract us from spiritual readiness for eternity. The parable works well as such an illustration because of the common sense of it. Proverbs 31 praises the Excellent Woman for this same common sense.

Most of us are probably familiar with the saying, "saving for a rainy day," yet how many of us actually do it? How many of us are prepared for an emergency or a disaster? Financial advisors such as Larry Burkett have always counseled believers with a common sense approach to their finances, including budgeting for living expenses, giving, saving, getting out of debt, as well as for emergency preparedness (illness, death, job loss).

The Proverbs 31 Woman knew how to handle her money. She knew how to make it and how to spend it. Even so, it wasn't the possession of money that made her truly excellent, it was her attitude toward it.

Skilled With Her Hands

She stretches out her hands to the distaff,
And her hands grasp the spindle.
                              Prov. 31:19

Perhaps the greatest difficulty in understanding this verse is in the unfamiliarity of the objects mentioned: the distaff and spindle. Most of us may recall Sleeping Beauty who, in accordance with a curse, pricked her finger on a spindle of a spinning wheel. That might give us some indication that a spindle is a long pointed object used for spinning yarn. But what about a distaff? What is that?

The frontispiece (page ii) is from a painting entitled *Lullaby* by William Adolphe Bougeureau (1825-1905). It was painted in 1875 and shows how the spindle and distaff were used. Near the baby's head the woman holds the spindle. The yarn she has spun is wound around it. In her other hand is the distaff. The distaff holds the unspun fiber, commonly flax, because the flax fibers are very long and difficult to control. Flax yarn is called linen.

We first saw the Proverbs 31 Woman's interest in the textile arts when we looked at verse 13.

She looks for wool and flax,
And works with her hands in delight.
                              Prov. 31:13

Now we learn what she delights in doing, spinning her wool and flax into yarn. Her yarns are used to make various fabrics for her home and family (verses 21 and 22), and to sell (verse 24). While this may not be profoundly spiritual, I think it points to an important principle.

Encourage The Young Women

There is an error in modern Christian thinking regarding how we judge one another's spirituality. There is a human tendency to want to classify our activities according to one of two categories: spiritual or secular. We believe that what is done at and for the church (preaching, teaching, ushering, tithing, visitation, VBS, nursery duty, etc.), is spiritually more important than what we do elsewhere. Consequently, we tend to judge others' spirituality by how much time they spend at church, and we esteem church ministry careers as more important than so called secular careers.

But is that how God views things? I say no. Why? Because God did not create a body of believers first, He created a couple: husband and wife, to whom He gave stewardship of the earth. While the church is the community of believers, the basic spiritual unit is husband and wife.

This is this significant because we need to understand that our day to day activities are how we truly live out our faith. Our testimony to the world is in how we live our lives outside the church, not how many times we go to church. The church's impact on the world is not in how many folks attended last week, but in the influence its membership has on the community in their daily living.

In reading Proverbs 31:10-31, we see this spiritual principle given as fact. Nowhere do we see a list of the Excellent Woman's religious activities. Why not? Because her most powerful ministry is to her family and home.

> *An excellent wife, who can find?*
> *For her worth is far above jewels.*
> Prov. 31:10

Skilled With Her Hands

> Excellent. Strong's #2428, חיל, *chayil* - a force, whether of men, means, or other resources. To be firm, or strong. An army, wealth, virtue, valor, might, strength, power.

God's inspired, inerrant Word describes an excellent and perfect wife as a homemaker, not as a leader in the church. Why? Because her God-given ministry is her family and home. It is the woman who sets the tone in the home and thus influences her entire household. She creates a stable refuge from the pressures of the world for her husband and children, and she uses her spiritual gifts to train and mature the next generation to impact the world for Christ.

Sadly, we are in a day and age where one's house is no longer the center and stability of family life. Instead, it has become merely an investment. Consequently, it is just a place to keep one's personal possessions, collect one's mail, and get a few hours of sleep and a quick bite to eat before rushing off to work, church, school, football practice, piano lessons, ballet rehearsal, garden club, etc.

Many women joke that they aren't domestically inclined because they don't know how to sew on a button, or that they could burn even water. However, the excellent qualities of the Proverbs 31 Woman are learned skills. She started at the same skill level that all women do, but she learned and developed these to a master skill level. Are we not capable of doing the same?

My exhortation to Christian women today is to set aside the world's wild goose chase to find "fulfillment" elsewhere, and to endeavor to see the ministry to their families as the most worthwhile and valuable ministry of all.

But godliness with contentment is great gain.   1 Tim. 6:6

Philanthropist

> *She extends her hand to the poor;*
> *And she stretches out her hands to the needy.*
> *Prov. 31:20*

So far we have seen that the Proverbs 31 Woman is a diligent worker who handles her money wisely. Because of these things, she is able to help others in need. She is an example of an exhortation we read in the New Testament,

> *Rather let him labor, performing with his own hands what is good, in order that he may have something to share with him who has need.*
> *Ephesians 4:28b*

While almost all Christians would agree with this principle, it doesn't seem to be commonly practiced. It is a sad fact that both tithing and donations to charities are down. But if we understand giving to be good, why is that so?

One reason Christians are unable to give freely is because their money is tied up in debt. The problem with debt is that it gives someone else the rights to our money, even before we earn it. That problem makes a good point of the following verse,

> *Owe nothing to anyone except to love one another;*
> *for he who loves his neighbor has fulfilled the law.*
> *Rom. 13:8*

We are unable to love our neighbor by meeting his needs if our money is tied up in debt.

Another reason giving is down, I think, is because we live in a day and age where people expect government to take care of all social problems including poverty. Our "giving" is in the form of taxes. Scripture, however, never endorses this. Rather, we are to help the poor. We see quite a few exhortations and examples of this in Scripture:

> And in the proportion that any of the disciples had means, each of them determined to send a contribution for the relief of the brethren living in Judea. Acts 11:29

> For Macedonia and Achaia have been pleased to make a contribution for the poor among the saints in Jerusalem. Rom. 15:26

> Zaccheus stopped and said to the Lord, "Behold, Lord, half of my possessions I will give to the poor." Luke 19:8a

> On the next day he took out two denarii and gave them to the innkeeper and said, 'Take care of him; and whatever more you spend, when I return I will repay you.' Luke 10:35

> Now in Joppa there was a disciple named Tabitha (which translated in Greek is called Dorcas); this woman was abounding with deeds of kindness and charity which she continually did. Acts 9:36

> He who despises his neighbor sins, but happy is he who is gracious to the poor. Prov. 14:21

> For I testify that according to their ability, and beyond their ability, they gave of their own accord, begging us with much urging for the favor of participation in the support of the saints. 2 Cor. 8:3-4

Philanthropist

> *He who oppresses the poor reproaches his Maker, but he who is gracious to the needy honors Him.*   Prov. 14:31

If we want to show others the love of God, then this is something we need to do.

> *But whoever has the world's goods, and sees his brother in need and closes his heart against him, how does the love of God abide in him? Little children, let us not love with word or with tongue, but in deed and truth.*   1 John 3:17-18

If we feel financially unable to help the needy, then perhaps it is time to take spiritual inventory regarding our money and our possessions. Budgeting even a small amount of money for this kind of giving honors the Lord and helps create our spiritual legacy.

> *Do not lay up treasures for yourselves treasures upon earth, where moth and rust destroy, and where thieves break in and steal. But lay up for yourselves treasures in heaven, where neither moth nor rust destroys, and where thieves do not break in or steal; for where your treasure is, there will your heart be also.*   Matt. 6:19-21

Faithfully Prepared

She is not afraid of the snow for her household,
For all her household are clothed with scarlet.
                                                    Prov. 31:21

It seems to me that we can glean two points from this verse: the first one obvious, the second one implied. Let's start by examining the word "afraid".

> Afraid. Strong's #3372, ירא, *yare'* – to fear, revere, be afraid; to be fearful, be dreadful, be feared; to make afraid, terrify

Why is the Proverbs 31 Woman not afraid? Because she is prepared. No matter how severe the winter may be, her household is ready for it. I'm not entirely certain why being clothed in scarlet provides a sense of security, but the point is that she has no reason to worry.

In a spiritual sense we should ask, "In what does her confidence really lie?" She may not be afraid for one of two reasons. Either her sense of security is in her own abilities or, having done all that she has been given to do, she trusts in the Lord for the outcome. How can we know which one? After all,

> "God helps those who help themselves."

Right? Wrong! Though often quoted as being from the Bible, this so-called verse is in fact not biblical. Various forms of it can be traced back to early Greek literature, but the most famous version is from Benjamin Franklin's 1757 *Poor Richard's Almanac*[1].

Encourage The Young Women

God helps them that help themselves.
Benjamin Franklin

But is this a biblical concept? Any student of the Bible and true believer should be quick to point out that trusting in self negates faith. In fact, the Bible admonishes us not to do so -

He who trusts in his own heart is a fool.
Prov. 28:26a

Does that mean that we should relax at our ease, do nothing, and assume that the Lord will take care of us in any disaster that comes our way? That extreme isn't biblical either. As Scripture says,

Make it your ambition to lead a quiet life and attend to your own business and work with your hands, just as we commanded you; so that you may behave properly toward outsiders and not be in any need. 1 Thes. 4:11-12

Our lifestyle is our testimony to those outside the church. In addition to being able to help those in need, our preparedness is a demonstration of our faithful obedience.

Who then is the faithful and sensible servant whom his master put in charge of his household to give them their food at the proper time? Blessed is that servant whom his master finds so doing when he comes. Matt. 24:45-46

As we saw in "Skilled With Her Hands", our spirituality is not based on our involvement with the church, but rather on the way we live our lives. Women have specific God-given responsibilities for their families and homes. This is, in fact, one of the most important ministries we are given. This is the work that the Lord expects us to be doing. It is not inferior or nonspiritual work, it is excellent work.

This brings us to the other reason that the Excellent Woman may not be afraid; because she has been faithful in her ministry to her family. How do we know that this is the reason? Because of verse 30:

> *Charm is deceitful and beauty is vain,*
> *But a woman who fears the Lord, she shall be praised.*
> Prov. 31:30

The Proverbs 31 Woman is praised because she reveres the Lord.

Two things please the Lord: our obedience -

> *He who has My commandments and keeps them, he it is who loves Me; and he who loves Me shall be loved by My Father, and I will love him, and will disclose Myself to him.*
> John 14:21

- and our faith.

> *Without faith it is impossible to please Him.*   Heb. 11:6a

These are not opposites, but go hand in hand. It is our faith which enables us to obey God's Word, even when our circumstances, feelings, or the world prod us otherwise. The Proverbs 31 Woman is an excellent example of faith and obedience working together. And it's not without reward.

> *Her children rise up and bless her;*
> *Her husband also, and he praises her, saying;*
> *"Many daughters have done nobly,*
> *But you excel them all."*

Encourage The Young Women

Charm is deceitful and beauty is vain,
But a woman who fears the Lord, she shall be praised.
Give her the product of her hands,
And let her works praise her in the gates.

Prov. 31:28-31

---

[1]*Familiar Quotations: A Collection of Passages, Phrases, and Proverbs Traced to Their Sources in Ancient and Modern Literature* Compiled by John Bartlet, online edition. http://www.bartleby.com/100/245.2.html

Takes Care Of Her Appearance

She makes coverings for herself;
Her clothing is fine linen and purple.
                                    Prov. 31:22

I have read this verse many times, but never actually studied it. When I did, I was surprised. I had always assumed that "coverings" referred to the Excellent Woman's garments. In doing my word studies for this verse, I discovered that it does not.

> Makes. Strong's #6213, עשה, *asah* - to do, fashion, accomplish, make
>
> Coverings. Strong's #4765, מרבד, *marbad* - [from the verb *rabad* (Strong's 7234) meaning to spread], spread (as in bedspread), coverlet.

If we refer back to the previous verse,

She is not afraid of the snow for her household,
For all her household are clothed with scarlet.
                                    Prov. 31:21

then we might say that the coverings for her bed are part of her preparedness for winter.

The verb "makes" doesn't give us any clue as to how they are made. Although the King James Version translates *marbad* as "coverings of tapestry" both here and in Prov. 7:16, the Hebrew word itself doesn't necessarily imply this. It is interesting to note that a derivative of this word is used to describe God's own works of creation as well as the miracles He performed on Israel's behalf. From that we catch the idea of the creative process involved.

Culturally, we can assume that the cloth for the coverings was woven and then sewn. We have already seen the Proverbs 31 Woman as a handspinner, but besides the added "tapestry" in the King James translation, no weaving terms are used in the passage. We don't know if she wove the cloth herself, or had someone else do it.

The second half of verse 22 addresses coverings of a different kind - her clothing.

> Clothing. Strong's #3830, לבש, or לבוש, 'lebush' - clothing, garment, apparel, raiment
>
> Fine linen. Strong's #8336, ששׁי or שׁשׁ, shesh or shaysh - something bleached white, linen, fine linen, marble, silk. Translated only once (Prov. 31:22) as "silk" in the KJV.
>
> Purple. Strong's #713, ארגמן, 'argaman - purple, red-purple (either the color or the dyed goods). Due to its cost as a dye, it is associated with royalty or the favor of royalty, nobility, the priests, and the temple.

In Proverbs 31, the word "clothing" is used both literally (here) and symbolically (verse 25). According to *Theological Wordbook of the Old Testament*,[1] the word *lebush'* implies more than just articles of clothing. It also assumes that clothing reveals something about the wearer: rank, status, or circumstance. We all understand this intuitively. In spite of the fact that we are taught from an early age, "Don't judge a book by its cover," we all know that our appearance does indeed make an impression on others and says something about ourselves. In that sense, our appearance becomes a social tool.

Takes Care Of Her Appearance

We live in a day and age where casualness has gone to an extreme. We are casual in our manners, in our attitudes, and in how we dress. This is unfortunate considering the emphasis on "self-esteem" which is being taught in our schools. Our personal grooming habits and choice of clothing announce to others how we really esteem ourselves. A slovenly or inappropriate appearance may demand to be accepted on the basis of "this is me, like it or lump it," but it still leaves that person subject to a negative impression on others and the consequences which stem from it.

True self-respect takes care of oneself and one's appearance. It takes the time to be neat, clean, and appropriately dressed. Why? Because true self-respect is not based on demanding acceptance from others; rather, it is based on the knowledge that

I am fearfully and wonderfully made.   Psalm 139:14a

The truth of this verse should set us free from needing to prove ourselves to the world, and empower us to get on with more purposeful living.

As Christian women, we need to understand something else. We need to understand that we are representatives of Christ to our families, our neighbors, our communities, and beyond. Because of this we should not be dressing so as to call attention to ourselves and our bodies, but we should dress so as to glorify (reflect) the One whom we represent.

The Proverbs 31 Woman was not haughty with her wealth, but generous. She understood both her place as well as her responsibility to society. She took care with her appearance. But the real impression she made was not one of stylish dress; rather, this is what is said about her -

Strength and dignity are her clothing,
And she smiles at the future.   Prov. 31:25

[1]*Theological Wordbook of the Old Testament*, Vol. I. Laird, Archer, & Waltke, (Moody Press, Chicago, 1980) 469

Unity in Marriage

Although we have focused almost exclusively on the Proverbs 31 Woman so far, we do get glimpses of her husband as well.

> *The heart of her husband trusts in her,*
> *And he will have no lack of gain.*
> *She does him good and not evil*
> *All the days of her life.*
>
> Prov. 31: 11-12

> *Her children rise up and bless her;*
> *Her husband also, and he praises her.*
>
> Prov. 31:28

What do we see about their relationship in these verses?

∼ He trusts her
∼ He is able to focus on providing for the family rather than domestic problems
∼ She treats him very well
∼ She has earned his praise

In verse 23, we get to know a little about what he does.

> *Her husband is known in the gates,*
> *When he sits among the elders of the land.*
>
> Prov. 31:23

To get a clearer understanding, let's take a look at a couple of words in this verse.

Known. Strong's #3045, ידע, *yada'* - acknowledged, recognized

Gates. Strong's #8179, שער, *sha'ar* - gate, entrance, space inside a gate, marketplace, court, public meeting place

Sits. Strong's #3427, ישב, *yàshab* - properly to sit down, specifically as judge, in ambush, or in quiet; remains, stays

Elders. Strong's #2205, זקן, *zàqèn* - aged, ancient men, elders, senators, those having authority

Let's look up several cross references too.

You shall appoint for yourself judges and officers in all your towns which the LORD your God is giving you, according to your tribes, and they shall judge the people with righteous judgment.   Deut. 16:18

All the people who were in the court (sha'ar or gate), and the elders, said, "We are witnesses."   Ruth 4:11a

Do not rob the poor because he is poor,
Or crush the afflicted at the gate;
For the LORD will plead their case
And take the life of those who rob them.   Prov. 22:22-23

In putting all this together, it seems likely that the Proverbs 31 Woman's husband is in a publically recognized position of authority as a judge.

Unity in Marriage

It was once a common saying that behind every good man there is a good woman. That concept has pretty much been thrown out the window in a day and age when women are focusing on their own careers rather than on their homes and families. I can understand this in part, because our world sees earning money as more important than raising children or governing a household without pay. Yet this is worldly thinking, which ignores a very important biblical fact: that husband and wife are one flesh (Gen. 2:24). Between them, they govern their life together. Each spouse is free to attend to his or her own areas of authority and responsibility, confident that the other is doing the same. They are a team.

There are many facets in life. In marriage, we see that the Excellent Woman's priority is the home; her husband's is the community. They are successful and prosperous because of the mutual respect and trust they have for one another. Neither one tries to be a whole unto themselves. It is as one flesh that they are individually strongest. United, they have a powerful impact upon society, though in different ways.

For Christian women, Prov. 31:10-31 lays out a goal to which we can aspire. For Christian men, it lays out

~ What to look for in a wife
~ What kind of woman he needs to encourage his wife to be.

It also gives him an idea of how they should function as a couple; his wife is not to rule over, his wife is to rule with. A biblical marriage means being two unique and individual parts of a whole. The whole is a life and ministry together.

Successful Busineswoman

She makes linen garments and sells them,
And supplies belts to the tradesmen.

Prov. 31:24

One thing this verse does is to settle the argument as to whether or not it is biblical for women to work. We know from verse 16, that the Proverbs 31 Woman had her own earnings and invested them. Now verse 24 gives us a better idea of how she got her earnings.

From verse 13, we learned that the Excellent Wife enjoyed working with fibers and textiles. From verse 19, we also learned that linen (from which she makes garments) is made from one of the fibers mentioned - the flax plant. Now we learn that she earns her money through these same pursuits, by making garments of linen and belts which she sells through local merchants.

We also know from verse 18 that she knew how to handle her finances wisely. It would seem that all of these things together put the Proverbs 31 Woman into the mythical "Superwoman" status of having it all, with success in both family and career. So how does she do it?

First, she knows her priorities and organizes her day accordingly.

She rises also while it is still night,
And gives food to her household
And portions to her maidens.

Prov. 31:15

Her day begins before sunup and the first thing she tends to is the needs of her household. The fact that she meets them is seen later in verse 28.

> *Her children rise up and bless her;*
> *Her husband also, and he praises her.*
>
> Prov. 31:28

There would be no blessings and praises if she neglected her family and their needs.

We also know that her business is not a point of contention between her and her husband. Rather, she has his respect and trust.

> *The heart of her husband trusts in her.* Prov. 31:11

The other key to her success, I think, is that she has a home business. Why is that important? Because, for one thing, it is one of the most time-efficient jobs one can have. Consider the amount of time most folks have to allow for travel to and from work. Then consider how time crunched many people feel, especially working women.

A home business is also efficient financially. If she based her business elsewhere, she would have overhead, childcare, transportation, and other costs (such as wardrobe and meals) which she doesn't have by working out of her home.

Most importantly, her home business makes her available for the management and guardianship of her home, as well as for the needs of her family. For example, have you ever been caught between having to care for a child too sick to go to school or daycare, and a boss who is pressuring you because you are badly needed at work? I have. It is a very stressful, lose/lose situation to experience.

Combine these two factors with a willingness to work hard, and we see the keys to the Proverbs 31 Woman's success. Is it possible for the rest of us? I can't answer that. But the Bible shows us that it is possible, and through the Proverbs 31 Woman, we have a model to consider.

No Fear

Strength and dignity are her clothing,
And she smiles at the future.
                                        Prov. 31:25

Although verse 22 tells us that Proverbs 31 Woman dresses well and takes care of her appearance, we learn here that the important things about her appearance are inner qualities.

> Strength. Strong's #5759, עוז or עז, *oze* - boldness, loud, might, power, strength, strong. Can refer to material, physical, social, or political strength.

We studied this word previously, in "Woman of Strength" (Prov. 31:17), where we learned that it also implies strength of character.

> Dignity. Strong's #1926 הדר, *hadar* - magnificence, that is, ornament or splendor: beauty, comeliness, excellency, glorious, glory, goodly, honor, majesty

We also studied the word "dignity" when we looked at Titus 2:3-5, "Dignity: A Basic Human Right?" We learned that in the Greek, "dignity" is a quality which inspires reverence and awe. It refers to a self-respect, not stoically never cracking a smile. From the Hebrew word above, we get a much broader sense of how that applies to the Proverbs 31 Woman.

> Clothing. Strong's #3830, לבש or לבוש, *'lebush'* - clothing, garment, apparel, raiment

We took a look at this word also, when we studied Prov. 31:22, "Takes Care Of Her Appearance". At that time we learned that the word "clothing" can be symbolic as well as literal.

The New Testament makes similar allusions. Consider these verses:

> *And let not your adornment be merely external — braiding the hair, and wearing gold jewelry, or putting on dresses; but let it be the hidden person of the heart, with the imperishable quality of a gentle and quiet spirit, which is precious in the sight of God.* 1 Peter 3:2-3

But can a person have dignity and strength, and be gentle and quiet? Absolutely. How is that? Because true self-confidence doesn't need to prove itself to anyone. It's not what comes out of a woman's mouth that commends her, it's her attitude.

Even though we know that the Proverbs 31 Woman dresses expensively, we see that biblically, it's not what's on the outside that makes her excellent; it's what's on the inside. The Excellent Woman wears her self-confidence and self-respect like a suit of clothes. They are obvious to everyone who sees her.

What else does the verse tell us about her?

> *And she smiles at the future.* Prov. 31:25b

Smiles. Strong's #7832, שׂחק, *sachaq* - to laugh, rejoice, play, mock

According to *Theological Wordbook of the Old Testament*, its use in this verse means "Of laughing in achievement ... The able and virtuous woman can live without concern and 'smile [rejoice, KJV] at the future' (Prov. 31:25) NASB"[1]

No Fear

"Future" is actually a two word phrase in the Hebrew:

> In time. Strong's #3117, יוֹם - *yowm* - literally a day, figuratively a time period defined by an associated term (in Prov. 31:25, "to come").
>
> To come. Strong's #314, אחרן or אחרין, *'acharown* or *'acharon* - behind, following, subsequent, western

Putting those two together, we might say, "A time period following the present." In other words, the future. In fact, the King James Version words it, "And she shall rejoice in time to come."

In this light, see this as an extension of her self-confidence. She has been faithful to work hard and the reward of this is freedom from worry and fear about the future.

---

[1]*Theological Wordbook of the Old Testament*, Laird, Archer, & Waltke, (Moody Press, Chicago, 1980) Vol II, p.763

Wise Teacher

*W*hat do powerful, successful women talk about?

> *She opens her mouth in wisdom,*
> *And the teaching of kindness is on her tongue.*
> Prov. 31:26

The Proverbs 31 Woman could use her position to promote herself, but she doesn't. She uses it to promote something else. Let's take a closer look.

> Wisdom. Strong's #2451, חכמה, chokmah - skillful (in war), shrewdness, wisely, wit, prudence, wisdom (in administration, religion, or ethics).

The book of Proverbs has much to say on the subject of wisdom.

> *The fear of the Lord is the beginning of <u>wisdom</u>,*
> *And the knowledge of the Holy One is understanding.*
> Prov. 9:10

> *The mouth of the righteous flows with <u>wisdom</u>.*
> Prov. 10:32a

> *When pride comes, then comes dishonor,*
> *But with the humble is <u>wisdom</u>.*
> Prov. 11:2

> *On the lips of the discerning, <u>wisdom</u> is found.*
> Prov. 10:13a

Encourage The Young Women

We see that what a woman says reveals much about her character. The Excellent Woman fears the Lord, is righteous, discerning, and humble.

> Teaching. Strong's #8451, תרה or תורה, *torah* - a precept, law, instruction, custom, or statute, especially the Decalogue or Pentateuch

Not only is the Proverbs 31 Woman wise, but she imparts that wisdom to others.

> *The lips of the wise spread knowledge.*
> Prov. 15:7a

> *The fear of the Lord is the instruction for wisdom*
> *And before honor comes humility.*
> Prov. 15:33

> *Older women likewise are to be ... teaching what is good, that they may encourage the young women ... that the word of God may not be dishonored.*
> Titus 2:3-5

> Kindness. Strong's #2617, חסד, *checed* - goodness, kindness, faithfulness, mercy

We studied the word "kind" when we looked at Titus 2:5. There, we learned how influential kindness can be. (See "Influencing Others")

> Tongue. Strong's #3956, לשנה, לשׁן, לשון, *lashown* or *lashon* - tongue. Used both literally, as the instrument of speech; and figuratively for speech, language, speaker

Wise Teacher

There is one who speaks rashly like the thrusts of a sword,
But the <u>tongue</u> of the wise brings healing.
Prov. 12:18

For every species of beasts and birds ... is tamed, and has been tamed by the human race. But no one can tame the <u>tongue</u>; it is a restless evil and full of deadly poison. With it we bless our Lord and Father; and with it we curse men ... from the same <u>mouth</u> come both blessing and cursing. My brethren, these things ought not to be this way.
James 3:7-10

Let no unwholesome word proceed from your <u>mouth</u>, but only such a word as is good for edification according to the need of the moment, so that it will give grace to those who hear.
Eph. 4:29

Who controls the tongue? We do. We have a choice not only in what we say, but in how we say it. The Proverbs 31 Woman exercises self-control when she speaks.

Do all things without grumbling or disputing; so that you will prove yourselves to be blameless and innocent, children of God above reproach in the midst of a crooked and perverse generation, among whom you appear as lights in the world.
Phil. 2:14-15

The Excellent Woman does not engage in gossip ("How Many Kinds of Gossip Are There, Anyway?"), complaining, or self-promotion. Rather, she encourages others and honors the Lord with the words of her mouth.

Time for reflection:

- What do I like to talk about?

- About whom do I like to talk?

- Am I in the habit of complaining?

- Do I enjoy arguing and taking issue with others?

- Am I quick to point out the faults of others?

- Am I quick to criticize?

- Do I like to make sure my opinion is heard?

- Am I quick to talk about my own experiences and opinions on any given subject?

- Do I really listen while others speak, or am I too busy thinking about what I'm going to say next?

- Am I comfortable being quiet? Or am I constantly running my mouth?

- Would others describe me as understanding?

- Would others describe me as kind?

- Do others seek out my advice?

- Would others describe me as wise?

Cause and Effect

The next several verses begin the conclusion to this passage.

> *She looks well to the ways of her household,*
> *And does not eat the bread of idleness.*
> *Her children rise up and bless her;*
> *Her husband also, and he praises her, saying:*
> *"Many daughters have done nobly,*
> *But you excel them all."*
>
> Prov. 31:27-29

We see two things here: what the Excellent Woman does, and what her family has to say about it.

What does she do?

> *Looks well to the ways of her household,*
> *And does not eat the bread of idleness.*
>
> Prov. 31:27

> Looks well. Strong's #6822, צפה, *tsaphah* - lit. to lean forward; by implication to look out or about, keep watch, observe, watch

This definition points to something we learned studying Titus 2:5: that a woman's domestic work is not being a mere housekeeper, but rather being a manager and guardian of one's household.

> Idleness. Strong's #6104, עצלות, *'atsluwth* - indolence, idleness, sluggishness, laziness

We already know that the Excellent Woman is not lazy. We can look back over the verses we have been studying and make a list of the action words which describe her. She:

Does – verse 12
Looks – verse 13, 27
Works – verse 13
Brings – verse 14
Rises – verse 15
Gives – verse 15
Considers – verse 16
Buys – verse 16
Plants – verse 16
Girds – verse 17
Makes – verses 17, 22, 24
Senses – verse 18
Stretches – verses 19, 20
Grasps – verse 19
Extends – verse 20
Sells – verse 22
Supplies – verse 22
Smiles – verse 25
Opens – verse 26
Teaches – verse 26

These are not the verbs which describe an idle woman. What does her family have to say about it?

> *Her children rise up and bless her;*
> *Her husband also, and he praises her, saying:*
> *"Many daughters have done nobly,*
> *But you excel them all."*
>
> Prov. 31:28-29

Cause and Effect

> Nobly. Strong's #2428, חיל, chayil - valiantly, virtuously, powerfully, efficiently, worthily; with strength, might, excellence

Chayil is the same word that was used in verse 10 to first describe the Proverbs 31 Woman:

> An <u>excellent</u> wife, who can find?
> For her worth is far above jewels.
> Prov. 31:10

The Proverbs 31 Woman's deeds and words have an impact on her family. She has been diligent in her ministry to them and the results are blessings and praise.

We should not be surprised. Cause and effect is a biblical principle:

> In everything, therefore, treat people the same way you want them to treat you, for this is the Law and the Prophets.
> Matt. 7:12

> Do not be deceived, God is not mocked; for whatever a man sows, this he will also reap. For the one who sows to his own flesh will from the flesh reap corruption, but the one who sows to the Spirit will from the Spirit reap eternal life.
> Gal. 6:7-8

> Now this I say, he who sows sparingly will also reap sparingly, and he who sows bountifully will also reap bountifully.
> 2 Cor. 9:6

To apply these verses, we have to ask the question, "What does my family say about me?" Do they praise me behind my back or complain about me? Do they see me as diligent, hard-working, and responsive to their needs? Or do I leave a lot undone, always making excuses for it?

As one whose children have now left the nest, I can heartily attest that the effort toward family and home is well worth it. The tendency is to grow weary with the responsibilities, so we need to keep in mind that it is only for a season. The physical, mental, emotional, and spiritual investment we make in our families today, will reap an eternal fruit.

Kingdom Minded

I'll never forget how shocked I was one day after my 51st birthday. I was checking out at the grocery store when the cashier (a woman who appeared to be about my age), asked me if I qualified for the 65 and older discount. In that nanosecond I realized something startling about myself.

Ever since I came to know the Lord, I've told myself that everything I did was for the Lord and that I didn't care what other people thought. A simple question concerning my age revealed something else. In the flustering minutes which followed that incident, I jumped to the conclusion that I needed to get rid of my gray hairs! Soon though, my initial emotional reaction dissipated, and I had to ask myself a question, which I'm going to turn around and ask you.

What motivates you? I mean at the barest, most basic level, what motivates you? Is it what others think? I have to admit that I'm constantly struggling with worry about how the house looks, how I look, and whether or not I've just said something stupid. Now, I'm not saying that keeping the house clean and myself well groomed aren't important. The question is, for whom I am doing it?

> *Charm is deceitful and beauty is vain,*
> *But a woman who fears the Lord, she shall be praised.*
> *Give her the product of her hands,*
> *And let her works praise her in the gates.*   Prov. 31:30-31

Verse 30 contains a contrast (notice that little word "but"?) It contrasts the way we behave and look (charm and beauty), with the condition of our hearts toward God.

> Charm. Strong's #2580, חֵן, *chen* - favor, grace, charm, elegance, acceptance

Being funny, clever, or charming is something that comes naturally for some people. It can also be learned to some degree. But beauty fades with age. Popularity is based on other people's whims, which are easily swayed. Prov. 31:30 tells us these things are vain.

> Vain. Strong's #1892, הֶבֶל, *hebel* - vapor, breath, empty, transitory, unsatisfactory

Beauty, charm, and popularity never last, which is why they are ultimately empty and unsatisfactory. We, however, are eternal beings who crave something of eternal worth. If we want to have a sense of lasting value in who we are and what we do, we should consider what qualities withstand the test of time. What was it for the Excellent Woman?

But a woman who fears the Lord, she shall be praised.
Prov. 31:31b

That word "fears" can mean to be afraid, but in this case, it does not.

> Fears. Strong's #3373, יָרֵא, *yare'* - morally reverent, afraid

This verse reveals the Proverbs 31 Woman's true source of motivation for everything she does in verses 11 through 27. It explains why the heart of her husband trusts in her. It explains why she is willing to rise early and stay up late. It explains why she is not afraid, why she smiles at the future, and why her children bless her and her husband praises her.

Everything the Excellent Woman does is for the Lord. Why? Because she respects and trusts Him. She understands that her sense of security and personal worth are not based on anyone else, nor on anything she can do. They are based solely on who the Lord is and what He can do. Consequently, she is free to live her life and enjoy her family without the burden of worry and fear of failure.

Time to reflect. What motivates you? Is it what others might think? What others might say? Do you often find yourself with a litany of "buts" and "what ifs" that continually parade themselves through your mind?

One day each one of us will receive the fruit of our hands.

> *Therefore we also have as our ambition, whether at home or absent, to be pleasing to Him. For we must all appear before the judgment seat of Christ, so that each one may be recompensed for his deeds in the body, according to what he has done, whether good or bad.*
>
> 2 Cor. 5:9-10

For Christians this is not a judgment for sin, but rather the reward for how we lived our lives. Appearing before the judgment seat of Christ is something that each and every believer will be required to do. This is where our works will "praise us in the gates" (Prov. 31:31).

When eternity comes, what will you have to show for your life? Will you be shown to have been like the Proverbs 31 Woman? I encourage you to take her example to heart.

The Excellent Woman: A Summary of Proverbs 31:10-31

Was the Proverbs 31 Woman a "real" woman? No, not as a biblical, historical character. Rather, she was an ideal woman, portrayed in a mother's advice to her son regarding what to look for in wife. For us, she is a standard to measure by, a role model to follow, a goal to work toward. We can read back over verses 10 to 31 and categorize a list of characteristics:

Her Character:
- Confident – v 25
- Courageous - v 17
- Dignified – v 25
- Diligent – v 14
- Early Riser – v 15
- Faithful – 21
- Generous – v 20
- Industrious – v 13
- Influential – v 10
- Kind – v 26
- Moral – v 30
- Not lazy – v 27
- Observant – v 27
- Organized – v 15
- Prudent – v 16
- Reverential – v 30
- Sensible – v 18
- Strong – v 17
- Trustworthy – v 11
- Well groomed – v 22
- Wise – v 16

Her Skills:
- Textile Arts -
    - Creative – v 13
    - Handspinning – v 19
    - Knowledgeable – v 13
    - Sewing skills – v 22

- Culinary Arts -
    - Purchaser of choice foods – 14
    - Supervises meals – v 15

- Management Skills -
    - Attention to detail - v 27
    - Common Sense – v 18
    - Home business – v 24
    - Investor – v 16
    - Observant – v 27
    - Organized – v 15
    - Overseer – v 15
    - Philanthropist – v 20
    - Prepared – v 21
    - Realistic – v 18
    - Stewardship – v 18
    - Successful – v 24
    - Teaches – v 26
    - Wise – v 26

Her relationships:
- With her children -
    - feeds well - v 15
    - trains in responsibility - v 15
    - clothes properly - v 21
    - looks after well - v 27
    - blessed by - v 28

The Excellent Woman: A Summary

With her husband -
- Appreciation – v 10
- Has his best interests at heart – v 10
- One of trust – v 11
- Praise – v 28
- Unity – v 23

Her Reward:
- the fruit of her own making - v 31

Did all these things come easily for her? Were they natural to her particular personality? Likely not. Each one of us is born naturally selfish. The ability to look to the needs of others requires self-discipline, it is a quality which must be learned. For the Christian, there is no question but that it must be learned. We are required to learn it.

> *A new commandment I give to you, that you love one another, even as I have loved you, that you also love one another. By this all men will know that you are My disciples, if you have love for one another.*
>
> *John 13:34-35*

The Lord is speaking here of *agape* love, the sacrificial love that puts the needs of others before one's own needs. This love proves we are His disciples. It proves we are Christians.

We can only speculate as to how easy or difficult these things might be to learn. But the fact that the Excellent Woman, even as an ideal, could be given as an example means it is possible. Therefore I challenge you, my sisters in Christ, to begin the journey toward becoming worthy of the title, "Excellent Woman."

Conclusion

The world is continually trying to pressure women into its mold. This pressure comes from all sides: radio, television, newspapers, magazines, movies, advertising, schools, governments, women's "rights" movements, often even the church. To live a life of true biblical womanhood is difficult, but not impossible. It requires keeping close to God's Word - to reading it, meditating on it, and practicing it. It requires courage, strength, faith, and prayer. It requires understanding that there are consequences for disobedience and a reward for our obedience, not only in this lifetime but in the one to come. With all my heart I encourage you, dear Women of God, to stay the course. Let the Word encourage you so that your example may bless and encourage others.

Bibliography & Resources

Bibliography

Bartlett, John, *Familiar Quotations: A Collection of Passages, Phrases, and Proverbs Traced to Their Sources in Ancient and Modern Literature* <http://www.bartleby.com/>

Franklin, Benjamin, *Poor Richard's Almanack*, Benjamin Franklin, Philadelphia, 1757

Harris, Archer, and Waltke, *Theological Wordbook of the Old Testament*; Volumes 1 and 2, Chicago: Moody Press, 1980

NET Bible. <https://net.bible.org/#!bible/Proverbs+31>

Strong, James, *The New Strong's Exhaustive Concordance of the Bible*. Nashville: Thomas Nelson Publishers, 1984

Vincent, Marvin R., *Word Studies of the New Testament*. Grand Rapids: Eerdman's Publishing, 1989

Vine, W. E., Unger, Merrill F., White, William Jr., *Vine's Expository Dictionary of Biblical Words*. New York: Thomas Nelson Publishers, 1985

Webster, Noah, *American Dictionary of the English Language, 1928 edition*. San Francisco: Foundation for American Christian Education, 1995

Wigram, George V., Green, Jay Patrick Sr., *New Englishman's Greek Concordance and Lexicon*. Peabody, MA: Hendrickson Publishers, 1982

Willis, Avery T., *Masterlife: Discipleship Training for Leaders*. N.p.: Sunday School Board of the Southern Baptist Convention, 1982

Zodhiates, Spiros, *The Complete Word Study Dictionary: New Testament*. Chattanooga: AMG Publishers, 1992

----*The Complete Word Study Dictionary: Old Testament*. Chattanooga: AMG Publishers, 1994

Encourage The Young Women

Resources

Books:
Arthur, Kay, *How To Study Your Bible.* Eugene, OR: Harvest House Publishers, 1994
McQuilkin, J. Robertson, *Understanding and Applying the Bible.* Chicago, Moody Press, 1983
Zuck, Roy B., *Basic Bible Interpretation.* Wheaton, IL: Victor Books, 1991

Websites:
Bible Dictionary <http://www.bible-dictionary.org/>
BibleGateway <http://www.biblegateway.com/>
BibleStudyTools.com <http://www.biblestudytools.com/>
Bible Toolbox < http://www.mybibletools.com/>
Biblica <http://www.biblica.com/en-us/bible/bible-versions/>
Christian Classics Ethereal Library <http://www.ccel.org/>
The HTML Bible <html. bible.com/index.html>
Hymnary <http://www.hymnary.org/>
Keepers of the Faith <http://www.keepersofthefaith.com/>
Linked Word Project <http://bible.worthwhile.com/bible.php?b=gen&c=1&v=0&d=1&w=0>
Lumina Bible Study <https://lumina.bible.org>
NET Bible <https://net.bible.org/>
Online Strong's Concordance & Bible Study Tools <http://christsassembly.info/research.htm>
Precept Ministries International <http://precept.org/>
StudyLight.org <http://www.studylight.org/com/>
The Unbound Bible <http://unbound.biola.edu/>
Webster's 1828 Dictionary <http://1828.mshaffer.com/>

Indices

General Index

References to names are to persons, not books of the Bible.
See the Scripture Index for specific scripture references.

A

abortion, 76
abuse, 87, 129, 130
accidents, 60
accountable, 64, 130
acknowledge, 198, 234
Adam, 150, 153, 163, 167, 168, 174, 175, 178, 179, 181, 183
addict / addiction, 13, 30, 32, 59, 64, 65, 99, 112, 113, 132, 136, 141, 144, 160, 180, 182, 196, 211, 213, 215, 231, 240
advertising, 259
affection, 53, 84, 144
affectionate, 83
agape, 12, 53-55, 68, 83, 139, 257
agreement, 52, 72, 84
Agrippa, 51
alcohol, 35, 71, 72
alcoholism, 72
alone, 48, 52, 58, 84, 109, 152, 153, 159, 161, 163
ambassadors, 102
angels, 172
animals, 152, 153, 179
appearance, 229-231, 239
application, 10, 13, 22, 23, 54, 69, 84

argument, 3, 4, 29, 101, 102, 119 156, 173, 178, 237
argumentative, 136
arrogant, 54
attitude, 13, 30, 32, 59, 64, 65, 99, 112, 113, 132, 136, 141, 144, 160, 180, 182, 196, 211, 213, 215, 231, 240
authority, 12, 108, 109, 129-130, 173, 174, 234, 235

B

baptism, 15, 68
Bathsheba, 187
beauty, 77, 227-228, 239, 251, 252
behavior, 4, 19, 20, 24, 29-32, 35, 36, 63-35, 67, 71, 72, 76, 93, 99, 104, 112, 126, 133-134 136, 139, 143, 144, 160, 176
belief, 3, 15, 48, 51, 52,, 97, 102
believe, 2, 3, 16, 25, 48, 52, 54, 76, 84, 89, 93, 98, 99, 101, 124, 130, 161, 165, 172, 181, 187, 218, 254
believers, 19, 39, 59, 102, 104, 183, 208, 215, 218, 226
beloved, 54, 106, 179
Bible study, 7-13, 25-28, 42
bioethics, 37

blame, 106, 168
blameless, 120, 128, 173, 245
bless, 198, 227, 233, 238, 245, 247, 248, 252, 253
blessed, 149, 152, 226, 258
blessings, 198, 212, 238, 245, 249
blind faith, 47-49
body, 19, 45, 52, 152, 155-156, 159, 165, 218, 253-254
bored, 198
boss, 21, 75, 198, 238
bride, 104, 179
bridegroom, 214
Bride of Christ, 208
budget, 204, 215, 223
Burkett, Larry, 215

C

Cain, 179
career, 156, 161, 164, 179, 198, 218, 235, 237
cause and effect, 249
character, 34-35, 38, 41, 58, 63, 72-73, 191, 196, 244, 255
charm, 227, 228, 252
childbirth, 175, 178, 180
childcare, 238
children, 12, 15, 19- 21, 23, 29-31, 58, 80, 81, 87-89, 91-95, 97-103, 108-109, 112-113, 116, 125, 128-130, 133-134, 136, 143-144, 157, 161-162, 164, 172, 175-177, 181, 191, 196, 198, 200-201, 219, 223, 227, 233, 235, 238, 245, 247-248, 250-252, 253, 256
Christ, 15-16, 21, 43, 47, 52, 55, 59-61, 72, 85, 102-106, 109, 111-112, 119-120, 124, 127, 129, 132, 156, 172, 180, 182-183, 208, 219, 231, 253-254, 257
Christian (defined 15-16), 25, 26, 30-32, 37, 43, 45, 53, 58, 63-65, 81, 94, 98, 101-102, 116, 121, 140, 165, 178, 184, 198, 199, 204, 218, 231, 235
Christianity, 47, 51, 55
Christlike, 36, 59, 127
church, 15, 23, 29, 35, 51, 57, 69, 81, 85, 88, 101, 104, 119-120, 125, 129, 131-132, 143, 145, 156, 165, 172, 181, 198, 208, 218-219, 226, 259
civil authority, 129
cleave, 91, 120, 155, 156
cloning, 37
clothing, 195, 214, 229-232, 239, 240
command, 13, 83, 97, 115, 119, 121, 168, 172, 226
commandment, 55, 105, 106, 200, 227, 257
commentaries, 7, 8, 12, 59, 187, 208
common sense, 67, 215, 256
community, 15, 218, 235
companion, 26, 68, 84, 152-153, 155, 159, 161

General Index

companionship, 84, 159-161, 163, 189
compassion, 214
conscience, 78, 112, 145
consequences, 4, 43, 48, 60, 71, 72, 107, 121, 129, 161, 168, 169, 175-183, 231
content, 192, 219
contention, 238
correction13, 75, 94, 95
counselor, 108
counterpart, 153, 163
Coverdale, Miles, 9
creation, 72, 77, 98, 149-151, 155, 175, 229
cross reference how to, 42
Cross, the, 48, 54, 83

D

Daniel, 149
Day of Christ, 60
deacons, 34, 38
death, 3, 48, 60, 94, 98, 168, 169, 176, 215
debt, 215, 221
deceive, 168, 171-174, 178, 181, 249
deceiver, 19
decisions, 4, 43, 84-85, 92, 125, 177, 193, 204
delight, 94, 171, 176, 195-197, 217
devil, 61, 67, 172
dignified, 37, 38
dignity, 37-39, 88, 232, 239-240
diligent, 78, 97, 176, 197, 199, 208, 211, 214, 221, 249-250, 255
diplomat, 108
disappointment, 93
discernment, 101
discipline, 41, 79, 88, 89, 93, 95, 97, 116, 176, 177, 257
discouraged, 79
discourager, 79
disease, 60
dishonor, 19, 41, 80, 107, 111, 115, 131, 133-137, 143, 243, 244
disobedience, 48, 51, 121, 126-127, 130, 139, 168, 174-175, 178, 181, , 183, 259
distaff, 214, 217
divorce, 60
doctrine, 13, 15, 45-47, 135
domestic, 87, 106-108, 130, 164, 197-198, 233, 247
domestically inclined, 107, 195, 219
don't judge a book ..., 230
dos and don'ts, 3
drugs, 35, 42, 57, 130

E

earn, 221, 233, 235, 237
earnings, 237
earth, 149, 150-153, 218, 223

Eden, 171
elders, 19, 29, 108, 143, 233-234
emotion, 33, 35-36, 43, 54, 57, 97, 143-144, 157, 168, 172, 175-176, 250-251
employee, 163
employers, 129
employment, 102
empower, 231
encourage, 19, 20, 22, 24, 29, 31, 63, 78-80, 83, 87, 103, 133, 134, 143, 161, 174, 235, 244, 254, 259
encouragement, 4, 80, 89, 97, 123
encourager, 64, 78
Enlightened Master, 15
entrust, 113, 127
environment, 102, 108, 196
equality, 107, 132, 164, 165, 182
error, 13, 218
esteem. 107, 121, 139, 145, 218, 231
eternal life, 48, 60, 212, 249
evangelical, 102
Evans, Dr. Tony, 51
Eve, 155, 163, 167-169, 171-172, 174-175, 178, 181-183
evil, 76, 112, 135, 140, 141, 168-169, 175, 178, 192, 212-213, 233, 245
excellent (see excellent wife/woman), 38, 157, 173, 189-190, 199, 208-209, 211, 215, 219, 227, 240
excellent wife/woman, 187-191, 197, 199, 200, 203, 205, 207-209, 211, 213, 215, 218, 227, 229, 235, 237, 240, 244, 245, 247, 249, 252-253, 255-257
exhort(ation), 13.39, 46, 198 219, 221-222

F

failure, 176, 253
faith, 32, 35, 37, 41, 45-49, 51-55, 57-61, 78, 85, 97, 102. 133-134, 143-144, 169, 174, 213, 218, 226-227, 241, 259
faithful, 34, 38, 213, 226-227, 241, 244, 255
Fall, the, 116
fallacy, 107
fallen human nature, 116, 177
fallen world, 60, 129, 176, 183
family, 12, 15, 21, 53, 72, 79, 107-109, 116, 125, 178, 197-199, 209, 214, 217-219, 227, 233, 237, 238, 247-250, 253
famine, 60
fear, 106, 119, 126, 139, 141, 176 190, 209, 225, 227-228, 241, 243-244, 251-253
feelings, 4, 7, 36, 53-54, 84-85, 121, 141, 169, 191, 224
fellow heir, 120-121, 124, 160

General Index

fellowship, 140, 189
feminism, 87
fine china, 121
fire, 60
flax, 195, 197, 217, 237
flesh, 91, 106, 120, 124, 152, 155, 156, 171, 178, 183, 235, 249
flood, 60
follower, 12, 21, 55
fool, 226
foolish, 94, 113, 176-177
forgiveness, 13, 48, 106, 194
Franklin, Benjamin, 225-226
free, 33, 34, 72, 104, 117, 128, 144, 208, 231, 235, 253
free gift, 48
free will, 169, 183
freedom, 4, 41, 182-183, 213, 241
freeman, 124
friend, 4, 10, 12, 21, 53, 57, 68, 79-81, 162, 181
friendly, 53, 83-84, 87
frivolous, 204
fulfill, 72, 87, 163-164, 174, 178, 199, 221
fulfillment, 91, 164-165, 192, 198, 219

G

gardener, 108
Garden of Eden, 171
garment, 108, 229-230, 237, 239
gentle, 34, 88, 144, 160, 240
gentleness, 89, 97, 121
gift(s), 48, 219
God, 3-5, 7, 9, 12-13, 39, 43, 47-48, 51-55, 57-61, 63-65, 68, 72, 76-78, 80, 83-84, 97-98, 102, 106, 108-109, 111-112, 115-116, 119, 123-124, 127-132, 135-136, 139, 144-145, 149-153, 156, 157, 159, 163-165, 167-169, 171, 174, 180-183, 192-193, 208, 212-213, 218-219, 223, 225-226, 229, 234, 240, 244-245, 249, 251, 259
  Son of, 15-16, 172
  Word of, 3-5, 7, 9-13, 19, 20, 41, 65, 78, 80, 107, 111, 115, 118, 131, 133-137, 143, 145, 183, 219, 227, 244, 259
God-given, 164, 219, 226
God helps those who help themselves, 225-226
godliness, 84, 93, 112, 176, 219
godly, 21, 113, 125, 144, 157, 183-184
gossip, 19-20, 24, 29-32, 34, 38, 63, 67-68, 71, 76, 133-134, 143-144, 245
grace, 9, 61. 68, 112, 120, 124, 180, 194, 245, 251
grapes, 156
guard, 39, 105, 107-108, 112-113, 120, 123, 130, 251
guardian, 107-109, 112, 130, 145, 189, 196, 198, 238, 247

H

head, 59, 108, 119-120, 125
helper, suitable, 84, 152-153, 159, 163, 165
help meet, 152, 163-165, 192
helpmate, 109
hermeneutics, 10
Holy Spirit, 4, 10, 80, 113, 127
home, 29, 41, 57, 91, 107-109, 111, 113, 130, 136-137, 162, 164, 191-192, 195-196, 198, 200, 209, 214, 217-219, 226, 235, 238, 250, 253, 254
home business, 108, 200, 238, 256
homemaker (also see keepers at home, workers at home), 107, 164, 195-196, 199, 219
homemaking, 198
homeschool, 15, 23, 97-101, 113
honor, 20, 116, 120-121, 135-136, 145, 160, 165, 223, 239, 244-245
honorable, 38, 103, 165
household, 88, 107-109, 120, 145, 172, 289, 198-200, 204, 214, 219, 225-226, 229, 235, 237, 247
housewife, 107
human, 3-4, 10, 21, 37, 54, 81, 98, 116, 120, 123, 149-151, 176, 180, 218, 245
humanity, 116
humility, 132, 182, 244

hurricane, 60
husbands, 12, 19-21, 29, 39, 41, 80-85, 87, 89, 103, 107-109, 111, 115-121, 124-136, 139-145, 157, 159-161, 167, 171-175, 178-179, 189, 191-196, 198, 200 218-219, 227, 233-235, 238, 247-248, 252-253, 257

I

idle, 68, 196,, 248
idleness, 198, 200, 214, 247
immodesty, 136
impulsiveness, 42, 136
inappropriate, 231
independent 4, 99, 109, 116, 159, 244
inductive Bible study, 149, 167
industry, 23, 179
industrious, 195-196, 204, 208, 211, 255
inequality, 115, 123, 131
inferior, 64, 124, 189, 227
inferiority, 115, 123, 159
innocent, 103, 126, 128, 245
instruction, 4, 19-21, 78, 88-89, 94-95, 97, 119, 188
interpret, 5, 8, 10, 12, 25, 28, 42 53, 76, 83, 123, 131, 149, 179
interpretation, 3-5, 9-10, 12-13, 23, 25, 42, 124, 179
invest, 204, 211, 213, 237
investment, 161, 219, 250
investor, 203, 205, 256

General Index

irreverence, 136
Israel, 156, 187, 230

J

Jesus, 7, 15-16, 21, 23, 47-48, 51, 54-55, 59-60, 72, 83, 105-106 111-112, 119, 124, 127, 129, 132, 168, 171, 181-182, 208, 212, 214
Jew, 8, 124
jewelry, 240
jewels, 189-190, 218, 249
joke, 140, 183, 199, 219
judge, 8, 21, 78, 119, 127, 164 218, 230, 234
judment, 43, 64, 181-182, 234 253
Judgment Seat of Christ, 253

K

keeper at home (also homemaker & workers at home), 107, 109
Keepers of the Faith, 23-24
keep house, 108
Kingdom, the, 121, 251
kind, 19-20, 29, 47, 54, 80, 84, 88, 107, 111-112, 115, 131, 133-134, 143, 145, 162, 192, 244, 246, 255
kindness, 89, 97, 111, 222, 243-244
knowledge, 9, 25, 30, 43, 47-48 51-52, 78, 80, 98, 101, 111, 121, 127, 140, 168-169, 175-176, 178, 231, 243, 244
Koine Greek, 25

L

laugh, 240
leader, 79, 104, 111, 115, 143, 219
leadership, 20, 23, 31-32, 63-65 72-73, 78-79, 88, 102, 123, 125, 127
Lemuel, 187-188
likeness, 36, 149, 151, 182
linen, 195, 217, 229-230, 237
Lord, 7, 9-10, 13, 42, 51, 54-55, 65, 72, 81, 84, 88-89, 91-92, 94, 97, 99, 106, 111-113, 116, 120-121, 127, 130-131, 141, 152, 156, 159, 163, 167-168, 171, 174, 178-179, 181, 194, 196, 204, 209, 222-223, 225-228, 234, 243-245, 225-253, 257
lord over, 20, 64, 117
love, 7, 12, 19-20, 22, 29, 32, 34-35, 37, 41, 45-46, 53-55, 57, 59-60, 68-69, 75, 78, 80, 83-85, 87-88, 91, 93, 95, 97, 99-100, 103, 105, 119-120, 123, 133-134, 139-140, 143-144, 156, 160, 165, 172, 176, 195, 198, 212-213, 221, 223, 227, 257
lovely, 38
lust, 33, 35, 171-172

M

magazines, 15, 164, 259

manager, 108, 145, 199-201, 247
mankind, 62, 72, 123, 150, 152, 183
marriage, 83-85, 91, 116, 119, 127, 129, 132, 139-141, 149-150, 155-157, 159-161, 165, 178, 181, 189, 192-195, 233-235
Master Life, 79, 81
masters, 15, 42, 72, 135, 208, 212, 219, 226
masters degree, 101
mastery, 99
maternal, 87-88, 144
men, 3-4, 19, 38, 55, 105, 107, 123-124, 129, 131, 156-157, 159, 164, 167, 172, 179, 182, 188-189, 219, 234-235, 245, 257
menial, 181
mental, 36, 52, 76, 87, 143-144, 168, 171-172, 207, 250
merchant, 196-197, 237
military, 116, 207
ministry, 81, 200, 209, 214, 218-219, 227, 235, 249
misquote, 167, 212
modest, 103, 126
money, 34, 163, 181, 190, 192, 203-204, 211-213, 215, 221, 223, 235, 237
movies, 7, 259
mutual submission, 119

N

Nebuchadnezzar, 149
neighbor, 21, 68, 221-222, 231
newspapers, 259
New Testament, 12, 24-25, 29, 33-34, 38, 41, 45, 47, 53, 63, 67, 83, 87, 94, 103, 108, 111, 115, 135, 221, 240
nursery, 218
nurture, 88, 94, 102, 160, 189, 193

O

obedience, 43, 51, 97, 169, 226-227, 259
obedient, 55, 60, 97, 169, 174
observation, 10, 13, 19, 34, 104, 164
Old Testament, 25, 479
one flesh, 91, 120, 124, 152, 155-156, 178, 235
oracle, 187-188
order, 19, 35, 72, 75, 78, 109, 115-116, 121, 123, 140, 143, 145, 152, 163, 175, 178, 221
orderly, 19, 35, 115, 123, 174
overseer, 19, 34, 41, 108, 156, 197

P

pain, 120, 175-179
passions, 33, 35, 41, 53, 83, 144
Paul, 13, 19-20, 34-35, 39, 42-43, 51, 53, 5-8, 69, 71-72, 77, 106, 143, 156
perseverance, 32, 35, 37, 41, 45-46, 53, 57-59, 133-134, 143-144

General Index

philanthropist, 108, 221-223, 256
Philippi, 39
Philippians, the, 59
Poor Richard's Almanac, 225
popularity, 251
pornography, 130
possessions, 164-165, 212, 215, 219, 222-223
postmodern, 77
power, 78, 107, 109, 189, 199, 203, 207-209, 213, 218-219
powerful, 81, 208, 218, 230, 239, 243, 249
prayer, 9, 43, 52, 57, 65, 68, 78, 80, 84, 94, 101, 120, 124
preachers, 7
preaching, 51
Precept Upon Precept, 9, 97, 100
prejudice, 115, 176
prepared, 164-165, 212 215, 219, 222-223
preparedness, 214-215, 226, 229
pride, 164, 171-172, 243
promises, 13, 106
Proverbs 31 Woman (Excellent Woman) 108, 187-189, 209, 213, 215, 217, 219, 221, 225, 227, 230-231, 233-234, 237-240, 243-245, 249, 251-255
prudent, 4, 31, 41, 213-214
punishment, 93-94

pure, 19-20, 29, 38, 41, 78, 103-107, 111, 115, 126, 131, 133-134, 143, 144
purity, 103, 105-106, 120, 173
purple, 229-230

Q

quiet, 127, 226, 234, 240, 246
quality, 33, 35, 58, 77. 239-240 257
quantity, 200

R

radio, 259
rejection, 4, 176
relativism, 75-77
repent, 13, 16, 48, 51, 106
repentance, 51, 194
representative, 151, 196, 231
resent, 178
resentment, 84, 160
responder, 172
reverence, 38, 121, 139, 194
reverent, 19-20, 24, 29, 31-32, 63-64, 67, 71, 76, 133-134, 143-144, 252, 255
revile, 112, 127, 135
Rich Young Ruler, 212
righteous, 13, 127, 234, 243-244
rights, 37, 164, 181, 188, 221, 239, 259
Robertson, Pat, 72
role model, 64, 184, 255

S

sacrifice, 54-55, 99, 198, 207
SAHM, 107
salvation, 47-49, 51-52, 127
Satan, 67, 84
school (also see homeschool) 23, 75, 99, 101-102, 125, 219, 231, 238, 259
secular, 119, 129, 218
security, 192, 213, 225, 253
Self, 35, 78, 93, 98
self-centered, 93
self-control, 33, 35-36, 41-43, 84, 113
self-discipline, 41, 93, 116, 177, 257
self-esteem, 231
selfish, 93-94
self-reflection, 106
self-respect, 38-39
seminary, 9, 101
sensible, 19-20, 29, 32, 35, 37, 41-43, 53, 56-57, 80, 103, 107, 111, 115, 131, 133-134, 143-144
serpent, 167-168, 171, 173, 175
sexes, inequality of, 123, 131
sexual, 53, 83, 103, 105
shrewd, 140, 203-204, 219, 243
sin, 16, 21, 48, 51, 57, 60, 68, 75, 77, 93-95, 103, 105-106, 127, 140, 144, 168, 178-181, 183, 208, 222, 254
sinful, 116, 183
sin nature, 164, 172, 176
sinner, 57, 178
skills, 28, 99, 101, 104, 217, 219, 243, 256
Sleeping Beauty, 217
slovenly, 231
smile, 232, 239-240, 248, 252-253
socialization, 99
society, 37, 75, 87, 164, 231, 235
Solomon, 187-188
Son of God, 15-16, 172
sorrow, 175-176
sound, 32, 35, 37, 41-43, 46-47, 49, 53, 55, 57, 133-134, 143-144
spindle, 217
spinning wheel, 217
spiritual, 120-121, 125, 127, 132, 150, 164, 171-173, 196, 212-214, 217-218, 223, 225, 250
spiritual gifts, 219
spiritual maturity, 29-30, 32-33, 36-38, 42, 57-59, 72, 72, 77, 102, 132, 143-145
spirituality, 218, 226
stay-at-home-mom, 164, 198
stereotypes, 172
steward, 150
stewardship, 213, 218, 256
strength, 61, 72, 95, 112, 175, 180, 189, 191, 207-208, 211, 219, 232, 239-240, 249, 255, 259

General Index

structuring scripture, 133-135
submission, 115-117, 119, 123-125, 129-130, 139
submit, 121, 129-130, 160, 172-173
superwoman, 237

T

tapestry, 229-230
teach, 7, 13, 20, 29, 32, 34, 41, 63, 77-79, 97-98, 124, 130, 132, 144, 176, 248, 256
teacher, 30, 64, 72, 75, 77, 101, 102, 108, 129, 143
teaching, 11, 19, 24, 29, 31, 45, 47, 63, 71-72, 76-77, 93, 97, 99, 133-135, 143-144, 167, 218, 243-244
team, 235
teamwork, 189
television, 7, 22, 72, 161, 259
temperance, 35-36, 41-42, 72, 123
Temperance Movement, 33, 35, 102, 108, 129, 143
temperate, 32-35, 37-38, 41-42, 53, 57
temptation, 68, 172, 181, 204
testimony, 85, 105, 218, 226
Timothy, 34, 77, 104
tithe, 52, 218, 221
train, 58-58, 79, 88, 94, 102, 109, 164, 176, 219, 256
training, 13, 101, 157, 176, 200

translated, 27-28, 34, 38, 41-42, 45, 103, 111, 126, 131, 151, 188, 191, 196, 203, 222, 229-230
translation, 12, 25, 33-34, 58, 67, 163, 230
treasure, 112-113, 198, 212-213, 223
Tree of Knowledge, 168, 178
Trinity, 156
trust, 47, 52, 55, 60, 68, 127, 130, 140-141, 169, 174, 181-182, 191, 193-194, 225-226, 233, 235, 238, 252-253, 257
trustworthy, 208, 255
truth, 3-4, 10, 13, 47, 54, 59, 78, 80, 98, 124, 135, 143-144

U

unbelievers, 183
undisciplined, 177
unemployment, 60
unfair, 127, 176, 188
unfulfilling, 196, 198
ungodliness, 113
unity, 156-157, 161, 165, 178, 191-192, 257
unkindness, 136
unrighteous, 54
unwise, 176

V

valor, 189, 219
value, 7, 67, 99, 107, 121, 139,

204, 252
VBS, 75, 218
vessel, 120-121
virtue, 63, 189, 219
virtuous, 240, 249
visitation, 218
volunteer, 101, 161

W
walk, 7, 10, 51, 60, 97, 106, 111
wasteful, 204
weak(er), 120-121, 172-173, 189
weakness, 120-121, 165
wealth, 190-191, 211-213, 219, 231
wealthy, 196, 197
weaver, 108
wife, 34, 41, 83-85, 89, 91, 93, 102, 108-109, 116-117, 120-121, 124, 130, 132, 155-156, 159, 161, 167-168, 173-175, 178-179, 188-190, 197, 199, 208, 218-219, 235, 237, 249, 255
wild goose chase, 219
willing, 9, 23, 48, 54-55, 121, 145, 174, 179, 195-196
wine, 19-20, 24, 29, 31, 33-35, 38, 42, 63, 71-72, 76, 133-134, 143-144
wisdom, 104, 187, 191, 243-245, 143-144
wise, 4, 171, 176-177, 181, 204-205, 208, 221, 237, 243-246, 255

wives, 83, 108, 113, 116, 119-121, 124-127, 129-132, 135, 139, 144, 157, 160, 173
woman (also see Excellent Woman, Proverbs 31 Woman) 119-120, 124, 143, 150-153, 159, 162, 167-169, 171, 174-175, 179-180, 184, 198, 205, 235, 237, 240, 248
women, 16, 19, 23, 30, 34, 69, 81, 87, 107, 111-112, 123, 128-129, 131, 140, 157, 159, 164, 167, 172-173, 178, 219, 226, 231, 235, 237-238, 243, 259
  older women, 19-20, 24, 29-33, 37, 47, 53, 58, 63-64, 67, 71-72, 76-80, 133-134, 136, 143
  younger women, 19-20, 24, 29-31, 41, 63, 79-80, 85, 87, 103, 133-136, 143, 200, 244
wool, 195, 197, 217
word study how to, 25-28
workers at home, 13-20, 29, 41, 80, 103, 107, 111, 115, 131, 133-34, 143-145
worldly, 113, 123, 235
worldview, 76, 97-98
worry, 175, 225, 241, 251, 253

Word Study Index

afraid 225	gentle 88
alone 159	gird 207
arms 207	good 77, 192, 211
behavior 63	hands 203
charm 252	heart 191
chaste 126	help 153
cleave .155	herself 207
clothing 230, 239	honor 121
considers 203	husband 131
coverings 229	idleness 247
covers 140	in time 241
deceive 171	keepers at home 107
delight 196	keep house 108
desire .179	kind 111
dignified 38	kindness 244
dignity 239	known 234
discipline 88, 94	leave 155
dishonored 135	likeness 151
elders 234	likewise 31
encourage 79	looks well 247
enslaved 71	love 53
everything 129	love their children 87
evil 192	love their husbands 83
excellent 189, 219	maiden 200
faith 47	makes 229
fears 252	makes strong 207
fine linen 230	malicious gossip 67
fruit 203	man 160
gain 211	manner 126
gates 234	meet 163

Encourage The Young Women

merchant 197	workers at home 107
much 71	works 195
nobly 249	
nor 71	
one 156	
oracle 188	
pain 175	
perseverance 58	
portions 200	
pure 103	
purple 230	
respectful 126, 139	
reverent 63	
rises 199	
rule 178	
sensible 41	
sits 234	
smiles 240	
sound 45	
strength 207, 239	
subject 115	
teaching 244	
teaching what is good 77	
temperate. 33	
tenderly cares 88	
to come 241	
tongue 244	
to their own 131	
trust 191	
vain 252	
wine 71	
wisdom 243	

Scripture Index

Genesis
1:26-27 151
1:26-29, 31 149-150
1:27 123
1:28 151-152
2:7-22 152
2:12-13 168
2:14-24 168
2:15-17 168
2:16-17 60
2:18 .... 84, 159, 163
2:18-20 152-153
2:20 163
2:23-24 155
2:24 .... 91, 124, 156, 235
3:1 167
3:2-3 .... 167, 178
3:4 172
3:6 .... 167, 171
3:13 .... 168, 171
3:16 .... 116, 175, 177-179
3:17-19 179
4:7 179

Deuteronomy
6:4 156
6:5-7 97
16:18 234

Ruth
4:11 234

2 Samuel
12:24 187

Psalms
119:18 10
139:14 231

Proverbs
1:1 187
7:16 229
9:10 243
10:1 176
10:13 243
10:32 243
11:2 243
12:18 245
13:24 176
14:21 222
14:31 223
15:7 244
15:33 244
17:25 176
18:18 94
18:19 193
19:18 176
22:6 .... 94, 109
22:15 .... 94, 176
22:22-23 234
28:26 226
29:17 .... 94, 176
31:1 187
31:4-7 188
31:8-9 188
31:10 ..... 189, 190, 218, 249
31:10-31 ...... 188, 189, 209, 218, 235, 255
31:11 .... 189, 191, 238

31:11-12 . . . . 140, 233
31:12 192
31:13 . . 195, 197, 214, 217, 237
31:14 . . . . 197, 199, 214
31:15 . . . . 199, 203, 214, 237
31:16 . . . . 203, 213, 237
31:16-18 211
31:17 . . . . 207-208, 239
31:18 . . . . 204, 211, 213, 214, 237
31:19 . . . . 217, 237
31:20 . . . . 200, 214, 221
31:21 . . . . 217, 225, 229
31:22 . . . . 217, 229, 239
31:23 233
31:24 . . . . 200, 217, 237
31:25 . . . . 230, 231, 239, 240, 241
31:26 243
31:27 . . . . 200, 214, 247
31:27-28 198
31:27-29 247
31:28 . . . 200, 233, 237-238
31:28-29 248
31:28-31 227-228
31:30 . . . . 209, 227
31:30-31 251
31:31 252

Song of Solomon
7:10 179

Matthew
3:8 194
5:28 105
6:19-21 223
6:24 . . . . 208, 212
7:12 . . . . 68, 249
15:14-30 213
19:16-22 212
24:45-46 226
25:1-13 214

Mark
10:17-22 212
10:21-22 212

Luke
1:37 193
6:31 140
6:45 112
10:35 222
18:18-23 212
18:27 127
19:8 222

John
2:5-6 172
2:8-9 172
3:16 54
4:2-3 172
13:14 181
13:34-35 . . . . 55, 105, 132, 257
14:21 227
15:22 21
16:13 10

Acts
9:36 222
11:29 222
26:20 51

Scripture Index

Romans
2:23-24 135
8:28-29 . . . . 127, 130
8:29 59
12:2 78
13:1 130
13:8 221
15:26 222

1 Corinthians
6:1 135
7:5 84
11:3 119
12:12-27 165
12:14,17, 22, 23, 25 165
13:4-8 54

2 Corinthians
5:9-10 . . . . 253, 254
6:16 - 7:1 106
7:11 . . . . 103, 105
8:3-4 222-223
9:6 249
10:5 . . . . 10, 43
11:2 103

Galatians
3:28 . . . . 121, 124, 171
6:7-8 249

Ephesians
2:10 111
4:15 . . . . 59, 80
4:28 221
4:29 . . . . 112, 245
5:21 119
5:22 . . . . 131, 132
5:22-30 160
5:22-33 . . . . 132, 139
5:24 129
5:25 132
5:25-27 . . . . 120, 173
5:28-31 120
5:30-32 156
5:31-32 84
5:33 145
6:4 88

Philippians
1:6 . . . . 60, 127
2:2 156
2:3-7 . . . . 132, 182
2:13-16 128
2:14-15 245
4:8 . . . . 38, 103, 105
4:19 52

Colossians
1:10 111
3:21 88

1 Thessalonians
2:7 88
4:11-12 226

2 Thessalonians
2:16-17 112

1 Timothy
1:5 78
1:10 45
2:3 35

2:10 112	2:4 . . . . . . 79, 83, 87, 97, 160
3:2 41	2:4-5 . . . . 80, 103
3:2-3 34	2:5 . . . . . 41, 107, 111, 115, 131
3:4 88	244, 247
3:8 38	
3:11 . . . . 34, 38	*Hebrews*
5:14 108	4:12 78
5:22 104	10:24 . . . . 22, 80
6:3 45	11:1 47
6:6 219	11:6 227
6:10 213	

2 Timothy

James

1:13 45	1:2-4 59
1:14 113	2:10 105
2:14 . . . . 78, 113	2:14 51
2:16-17 113	2:19 48
2:23-24 113	2:24 52
3:6 173	2:26 52
4:3 46	3:1 64
	3:7-10 245

Titus

	3:8-12 106
1:2 46	3:17 104
1:5 . . . . 19, 35, 143	
1:6 89	*1 Peter*
1:8 41	2:21-23 127
1:9 46	3:1 131
1:13 46	3:1-2 . . . . 126, 139
2:2 . . . 32, 35, 37, 41, 45-47,	3:2 104
57, 59, 143	3: 2-3 240
2:2-3 . . . . 37, 53, 72-73	3:7 . . . . 120, 124
2:2-5 133-139	3:16 112
2:3 . . . . . 27, 35, 58, 67, 71-72	3:17 160
76, 77	4:4 135
2:3-4 . . . . . 24, 29, 31, 53, 63	4:8 140
2:3-5 . . . . . 19, 29, 143, 183,	4:10 68
239, 244	5:3 . . . . 20, 64

Scripture Index

5:6-11 . . . . 61, 180

2 Peter
2:2 135

1 John
2:16 171
3:3 104
3:17-18 223

Revelation
21:1 60

www.ingramcontent.com/pod-product-compliance
Lightning Source LLC
Chambersburg PA
CBHW071858290426
44110CB00013B/1200